LIBRARIES AND THE ENLIGHTENMENT

Libraries *and the* Enlightenment

WAYNE BIVENS-TATUM

Library Juice Press
Los Angeles, CA

Copyright 2011 Wayne Bivens-Tatum

Published in March 2012 by Library Juice Press

Library Juice Press
PO Box 25322
Los Angeles, CA 90025
http://libraryjuicepress.com

Library Juice Press is an imprint of Litwin Books, LLC.

Printed on acid free, sustainably-sourced paper.

Cover image: Engraving by Johann Melchior Feseli, 1719, depicting the Bürgerbibliothek in Zurich, Switzerland, originally a church, converted to a public library in 1634.

Designed by Martin Wallace

Library of Congress Cataloging-in-Publication Data

Bivens-Tatum, Wayne.
  Libraries and the Enlightenment / Wayne Bivens-Tatum.
     pages cm
  Summary: "Traces the historical foundations of modern American libraries to the European Enlightenment, showing how the ideas on which library institutions are based go back to the ideas and institutions of that revolutionary time"--Provided by publisher.
  Includes bibliographical references and index.
  ISBN 978-1-936117-42-0
  1. Libraries--United States--History. 2. Academic libraries--History. 3. Public libraries--Political aspects--United States--History. 4. Libraries--Aims and objectives. 5. Libraries and society. I. Title.
  Z731.B655 2012
  027.073--dc23
                              2011043639

ACKNOWLEDGEMENTS

Even a short book like this could not be written without a great deal of support from others. The following heartily deserve my thanks and gratitude: Princeton University, for providing me with an excellent library to support my research and especially for providing the research leaves that allowed me to finish the book by the deadline; Richard and Mary Bivens, for their hospitality in allowing me to use their lakehouse as a writer's retreat for two summers in a row; Nazareth Pantaloni, for his excellent critical comments on the manuscript and for his willingness to challenge my own prejudices about the Enlightenment; Rory Litwin, for approaching me about writing something in the first place and giving me the incentive to work on a project I've been thinking about for a while; and last (but definitely not least) my wife Jennifer and my daughter Elizabeth, for putting up with long intervals of me ignoring everything but my books and my laptop.

CONTENTS

Acknowledgements v

Preface ix

The Enlightenment: A Brief Introduction 1

Academic Libraries and the Philosophical Enlightenment 47

Public Libraries and the Political Enlightenment 93

Universal Libraries: Dream and Reality 141

The Universal Library of the Enlightenment 185

Bibliography 193

Index 201

PREFACE

The philosophical and political principles of the European Enlightenment provide the philosophical foundation of American academic and public libraries. The values of the Enlightenment should seem very familiar to Americans. The Enlightenment belief that scientific investigation of nature and society leads to improvements and progress has been a constant American refrain since the early republic. American political rights are numerous: individual human rights, liberty, democracy, equality, the freedom to believe what you like, behave how you want as long as others are not harmed, study what you want, share your beliefs or insights freely with the world. These rights are commonplaces of American identity. Also derived from the Enlightenment is the belief in the necessity of education in a democratic republic and the obligation of the state to improve the lives of all its citizens, not just the lives of the rich and powerful. This book explores the relationship between the values of the Enlightenment and the development of modern American academic and public libraries.

Chapter I provides an overview of the Enlightenment, both as an historical phenomenon and as an ongoing political project. It explores Enlightenment thought through the work of key eighteenth-century thinkers as well as the work of contemporary historians and philosophers. The chapter investigates both the philosophical or scientific principles of the Enlightenment as well as the political principles and develops an interpretation of the Enlightenment relevant to the history of libraries.

Chapter II traces the influence of the philosophical principles of the Enlightenment on modern academic libraries, especially research libraries. The belief that humans should pursue knowledge for its own sake, subject that knowledge to criticism based on reason and evidence, scientifically investigate nature and culture, and freely publish the results of those investigations provided the impetus to found modern research universities and along with them the academic libraries necessary for their operation. Because academic libraries are by nature adjuncts to their institutions of higher education, much of Chapter II explores the history of higher education and the birth of the research university and the research library necessary for its operation. We move from the Enlightenment to the German Idealist movement and its influence on the founding of the University of Berlin, the world's first true research university. Then we follow the German Model of the research university as it slowly makes it way to the United States and significantly changes the nature of higher education and academic libraries in America.

Chapter III explores the influence of the political principles of the Enlightenment on the American public library movement. The knowledge created through unlimited research should benefit everyone. Useful knowledge should improve the lives of the citizens, because in a democratic republic all citizens are supposed to educate themselves to make wise political decisions, and a just society both educates its citizens and seeks to improve their lives. These goals derived from Enlightenment thought motivated the foundation of American public libraries. We see how a belief in the necessity of educating citizens of a free republic led to the establishment of public libraries throughout the United States, and how the shifting purpose of these public libraries has provided continual fodder for debate.

Chapter IV examines several examples of the dream of a universal library, including the Library at Alexandria, a seventeenth century French treatise on developing a research library, the *Encyclopédie* project in eighteenth century France, H.G. Well's idea for a "World Brain," Vannevar Bush and the Memex (a machine similar to but predating the modern personal computer), the influence of Google, and the recent call for a Digital Public Library of America.

This work is not a comprehensive history of its subject by any means. Any one of the chapters could expand into a book of its own, or even several books. Throughout this book, I have tried to focus attention on foundational texts and critical moments in the history of American libraries. In the following chapters, we see the development of the Enlightenment during the eighteenth century and the emergence of a coherent set of values centering on human reason and freedom. The values of the Enlightenment in turn provided the inspiration and philosophical foundation for American academic and public libraries, as well as the universal library they can potentially create. As American libraries developed, their mission to provide information equally to everyone rose in importance, and libraries as systems of cooperation and sharing moved ever closer to such universal access. This trend logically culminates in a universal library available to all, or what we might consider the Universal Library of the Enlightenment. The dream of a universal library is as old as the Library at Alexandria, and received fresh attention from the Enlightenment forward, as we will see. The Universal Library of the Enlightenment could actually exist, but only in cooperation with American libraries.

CHAPTER I

The Enlightenment: A Brief Introduction

WHAT IS ENLIGHTENMENT? In some ways the meaning of "enlightenment" should be clear. It means to illuminate metaphorically, to direct light onto something, usually with the purpose of understanding that thing. However, "enlightenment" seems to have as many meanings as there are people who seek enlightenment or seek to understand it.

One might think that the investigation of "enlightenment" would be easier with some qualifications. This book examines the relationship between libraries and *the* Enlightenment. The initial article and the capital E already narrows the field somewhat, but the Enlightenment can still have many meanings, and the scholarly debate about those meanings fills many volumes. In its most basic sense, it is considered an historical period, beginning sometime in the late seventeenth century or early eighteenth century, and extending to the late eighteenth century, perhaps running from the

English Glorious Revolution of 1688 to the French Revolution of 1789. The dates shift depending upon what one wants to emphasize. For example, the historian Jonathan Israel pushes the date back to 1650 and the writings of Spinoza and Descartes to emphasize the beginnings of what he terms the "Radical Enlightenment."

Among contemporary historians the Enlightenment is sometimes considered just an historical period, but the Enlightenment can also encompass the set of philosophical and political principles that emerged from this period in history, especially in France, England, and America. Sometimes this is called "The Enlightenment Project" to distinguish it from the eighteenth century historical period. In this book, I will also be addressing this sense of Enlightenment, the sense in which the principles that emerged among Enlightenment-era thinkers in certain countries changed the way people thought and governments acted from the eighteenth to the twenty-first centuries. Even this meaning of Enlightenment is contested by various scholars depending on their historical and philosophical approaches. Though I will be discussing the principles of Enlightenment in a positive way — in line with numerous historians and philosophers over the last 300 years — the past few decades have also seen a negative reaction to certain aspects of Enlightenment, or sometimes, as the philosopher Tzvetan Todorov noted in his recent book *In Defence of the Enlightenment*, to distortions of Enlightenment thought taken for the real thing.

Philosophical Enlightenment

Contesting the meaning of *enlightenment* in the philosophical, rather than historical, sense itself has a history, which provides a good place to examine the possible meanings. In the eighteenth century, people were aware that *something* was changing science, philosophy, and politics, and they were trying to understand what that something was. The search to understand the Enlightenment has yet to end.

For our investigation, let us begin with some passages from Enlightenment thinkers in the eighteenth century. Perhaps the most famous definition comes from Immanuel Kant's 1784 essay, "An Answer to the Question: What is Enlightenment?" A footnote in a 1783 article in the journal *Berlinische Monatsschrift* asked, "*Was ist Aufklärung?*" ("What is Enlightenment?"). Kant among others responded to the query. Kant's famous opening paragraph deserves to be quoted in full:

> *Enlightenment is mankind's exit from its self-incurred immaturity.* Immaturity is the inability to make use of one's own understanding without the guidance of another. *Self-incurred* is this inability if its cause lies not in the lack of understanding but rather in the lack of the resolution and the courage to use it without the guidance of another. *Sapere aude!* [Dare to know!] Have the courage to use your *own* understanding! is thus the motto of enlightenment (Schmidt 58).

To some, the injunction to use our *own* understanding seems so banal these days. Of course we use our own understanding and trust our own judgments. We are adults, after all. Who else's judgment would we trust?

Kant was writing in a different era when this line of thought was less commonplace than it is now. At the beginning of the eighteenth century, most countries or principalities in Europe had monarchs and established churches that controlled education and public expression. To judge by the difficulty with which enlightened views on science and politics fought against common opinion, many people must have deferred in their beliefs to the aristocracy or the church. They did not or could not use their own judgments about important matters of knowledge or morality, at least publicly. They relied upon the guidance of another, even when that guidance was inappropriate to the subject at hand, like arguing an empirically testable hypothesis purely on religious or political grounds.

Recall the early days of the scientific revolution, when the Catholic Church condemned Copernicus' heliocentric theory of the universe as false because it was contrary to scripture. This episode exemplifies an anti-Enlightenment attitude. The problem is not the correctness of Copernican theory. Contrary to the heliocentric theory of the universe, the sun is not in fact the center of the universe. Neither is the earth the center of the universe, as the Church's geocentric theory held. The question of truth is less relevant than the question of the criterion of truth. What counts as a fact about nature? As truth? Who gets to decide, and how do they make their judgments? For devout Catholics in the early seventeenth century, the Catholic Church decided what was or was not fact, and the criterion for truth was a rather literalist interpretation of the Bible, similar to some fundamentalist Christians today. Contrary to anti-Catholic propaganda then and now, the Church was not trying to suppress "truth," but was in fact trying to suppress error. However, the criterion for what counted as truth or error was inappropriate and irrelevant to the question under consideration. This error of reason was certainly not confined to the Catholic Church. According to Brian Silver in *The Ascent of Science*, the "*Protestant* churches on the Continent . . . took the lead in questioning the fruits of natural science. . . . Luther said of Copernicus, 'The fool wants to turn the whole art of astronomy upside down'" (53). Attitudes have now changed for many in the West — in those countries most touched and transformed by Enlightenment thought — and facts about nature are now decided by nontheological criteria of reason and evidence (with the obvious exception of religious fundamentalists). This is true even for the Catholic Church. Those influenced by Enlightenment thought believe that facts and theories about nature are decided by standards of scientific reasoning theoretically common to all human beings, not just to believers in a particular religion.

In science, or what the eighteenth century called "natural philosophy," human beings decide the truth for themselves based upon their own human judgments, which are always subject to criticism and challenge. This is partly what Kant meant. It is not necessarily that I, an individual human being, trust my individual judgment about every fact or hypothesis in the world. The world of truth is not contained within my mind, but neither do I hand judgment over to those whose expertise lies in other areas. I do not trust an evangelical Christian minister to tell me about evolution based upon his interpretation of the Bible, just as I would not trust an atheistic scientist to tell me about what religion means and has meant to human beings just because some religious tenets contradict scientific facts. I do not accept what politicians tell me about global warming based on their party platform, just as I would not trust the consensus of climate scientists on how to win elections or acquire financial support from lobbyists. This goes further, because using my own judgment I also do not simply accept the word of any given expert even on an appropriate field of expertise. Experts differ even amongst themselves, sometimes quite broadly and sometimes over minute details. If the subject were relevant to my needs, I could examine debates amongst the experts themselves and try to decide my beliefs based on the best arguments and evidence relevant to the question.

Consider another eighteenth century proponent of Enlightenment, the Marquis de Condorcet, on the utility of science. Though sometimes considered quite utopian and definitely enamored of the progress of science, Condorcet showed skeptical good sense in his approach. "Enlightened men" should search in all the sciences to bring them together, thus "they may form a judgment of their own efforts, ascertain the false steps they may have taken, preserve themselves from pyrrhonism as well as credulity, and even from a blind mistrust or too extensive submission to the authorities even of men of reputation and knowledge" (Kramnik 68). Trusting our human judgment means that we are all theoretically capable of judging the truth for ourselves, because the reasons behind the truth are accessible to all humans. Enlightened persons are not credulous enough to believe something merely because they have been told it is true or because of a tradition. Truth based upon tradition assumes that those in the past necessarily knew better than we do today about . . . well, about everything. Even in areas where it makes sense to depend upon tradition — and there are certainly such areas — tradition locks knowledge into a container we cannot examine. As Condorcet remarks, "being persuaded that the men of their time knew everything they would ever know, and would always believe that in which they then had fixed their faith; they confidently built their reveries upon the general opinions of their own country and their own age" (68). The enlightened trust their own judgments and the judgments of relevant experts, but even then they are skeptical and want to be persuaded by the best and most appropriate evidence. However, they are also not so skeptical about the possibility of knowledge that they abandon enquiry and submit to pyrrhonism. Knowledge is possible, but requires reason, evidence, and debate, and every claim can be criticized and challenged by the use of reason and evidence. Trusting our own judgment and reasoning about our own beliefs without simply accepting the word of an authority, and an inappropriate authority at that, requires a particular social attitude toward investigation, reasoning, and free expression rare in human history. It remains difficult today, and in the eighteenth century was even more difficult because the appropriate attitudes were just emerging in parts of Europe and America. One of the greatest intellectual projects of the eighteenth century was the *Encyclopédie, ou dictionnaire raisonné des sciences, des arts et des métiers*, published from 1750 to 1772, with Denis Diderot as the main editor. It sought to describe the entire world of knowledge of its time. Fittingly enough, Diderot — one of the leading *philosophes* or proponents of the Enlightenment in France — wrote the entry on "Encyclopédie" for the *Encyclopédie*. "I have said that it could only belong to a philosophical age to attempt an *encyclopédie* ... because such a work demands more intellectual daring than is commonly found in ages of pusillanimous taste. All things must be examined, debated, investigated without exception and without regard for anyone's feelings" (Kramnik 18). To many this may sound harsh; even within research universities supposedly dedicated to the pursuit of knowledge there are fields that pursue knowledge without regard to emotional or political objections and those that do not. Consider only the reaction to then Harvard University President Laurence Summers in 2005 when he "sparked an uproar at an academic conference . . . when he said that innate differences between men and women might be one reason fewer women succeed in science and math careers" (Bombardieri). Even some university professors consider some topics out of bounds for discussion or investigation. Nevertheless, this enlightened spirit of investigation and debate is crucial to the progress of any field of knowledge.

And not just a spirit of investigation and debate, but a spirit of openness as well. Investigation is sterile and debate impossible without openness and the freedom of expression. Diderot thought "it would be desirable for the government to authorize people to go into the factories and shops, to see the craftsmen at their work, to question them, to draw the tools, the machines, and even the premises" and that "there would be few secrets that one would fail to bring to light by this method, and all these secrets would have to be divulged without any exception." Why *bring to light* these secrets? So that we all may learn from them, so that we may all be *enlightened*. He mocks those who want to hide such secrets as "narrow minds, deformed souls, who are indifferent to the fate of the human race and who are so enclosed in their little group that they see nothing beyond its special interest." The narrow minds and deformed souls think such an encyclopedia of useful arts should be only "an enormous manuscript that would be carefully locked up in the king's library, inaccessible to all other eyes but his." But for the Enlightenment, knowledge was meant to be shared, not hoarded. The enlightened investigate, examine, debate, publish. They do not "spread darkness over [foreigners] or . . . plunge . . . the rest of the world into barbarism so that we [can] dominate more securely over everyone," nor do they "sacrifice the happiness of future ages and that of the entire human race" by hoarding our secrets instead of sharing them (Kramnik 19). The enlightened desire to increase knowledge to benefit not just themselves, but the entire human race.

This goal still drives the best scientific and philosophical thinking today, and it evolved during the Enlightenment, when the enlightened regarded Francis Bacon and Rene Descartes with great esteem, and could perhaps be said to almost worship Isaac Newton. Jean Le Rond d'Alembert — another principal editor of the *Encyclopédie* — in an introduction to that work remarks that "when the human mind emerged from barbarism, it found itself in a kind of childhood, eager to accumulate ideas" but unable to because it had not been taught how (Kramnik 7). Despite the darkness of the age, "the philosophic spirit took refuge in the writings of some great men" who "worked silently in the remote background to prepare the light of reason which gradually and by imperceptible degrees was to illuminate the world" (8). The main progenitors of this philosophical spirit trying to illuminate the world through the light of reason were Bacon, who "divided the sciences into branches" to investigate what was known about them and what was yet still to be discovered; Descartes, who through his skepticism cleared away intellectual rubbish and advanced both philosophy and mathematics; and Newton, who "gave to philosophy a method it seems obliged to retain" (12). Note Voltaire's comments about Newton in his *Letters Concerning the English Nation*: "Who was the greatest man? . . . If true greatness consists in having received from heaven the advantage of a superior genius, with the talent of applying it for the interest of the possessor and of mankind, a man like Newton . . . is surely by much the greatest" (52-53). Or perhaps more illustrative of the high opinion of Newton is Alexander Pope's exuberant encomium: "Nature and Nature's laws lay hid in night:/ God said, "Let Newton be!" and all was light." The common trait of these philosophical geniuses, and what earned enlightened esteem, was their desire to increase scientific knowledge and to bring reason to the study of science.

The organization of science we have today — with its amalgam of corporate, government, and university funding — was an almost unimaginable accomplishment in the eighteenth century. During the seventeenth and eighteenth centuries scientific investigation and publication were usually organized into academies and societies, with the hope that these would further progress and promote knowledge by funding research and publishing transactions. Joseph Priestly, who discovered oxygen, hoped that these societies would fund yet more research, and that scientists would divide themselves into smaller and smaller groups to experiment on increasingly more detailed questions, and publish "a periodical account ... of them all, successful or unsuccessful" (Kramnik 70), which is what research universities do today. Priestly believed not only that humans should act to increase and disseminate scientific knowledge, but that they should do so for the benefit of everyone. Scientific investigation is useful if practical, and beneficial because of the power we get over nature by the knowledge we gain of its laws, but also because makes human beings "more comfortable and happy." According to Priestly, "the greatest, and noblest use of philosophical speculation [or scientific research, as we would say] is the discipline of the heart, and the opportunity it affords of inculcating benevolent and pious sentiments upon the mind" (72). Scientific investigation and experiment were not ends in themselves necessarily, but were to benefit human beings and improve their lives. (Though as we will see in Chapter

II, knowledge might have to be pursued for its own sake for these benefits to accrue.)

The eighteenth century was an age of scientific discovery, even if eclipsed significantly by the nineteenth and twentieth centuries, and scientific investigators wanted to understand nature to make human life better. The American Philosophical Society, founded in Philadelphia in 1743 by Benjamin Franklin, eventually merged with the American Society for Promoting Useful Knowledge to become the American Philosophical Society Held at Philadelphia for Promoting Useful Knowledge, its title a perfect embodiment of an important Enlightenment goal. In numerous ways it was age of invention and the discovery of useful knowledge to improve the lot of humankind. The eighteenth century saw the invention of the piano, the steam engine, the mercury thermometer, the diving bell, the octant, the flying shuttle (for weaving, not space travel), the Leyden jar, the lightening rod, the Spinning Jenny, bifocals, the oil lamp, the power loom, and, the threshing machine. The enlightened sought knowledge for its own sake, but also to benefit humankind. The focus was not just on nature, but on society as well, on studying and reforming society for the benefit of all.

Along with the study of nature came the study of humans in society. The eighteenth century saw the emergence of economics, political science, psychology, and sociology. Everything could be studied and classified, and classify they did during the Enlightenment. In his celebratory *Empire of Reason: How Europe Imagined and America Realized the Enlightenment*, Henry Steele Commager lists enthusiastically various classification schemes originating during the Enlightenment. "They organized, they systematized, they classified, they codified, and all Nature, the universe itself, fell into order at their bidding. The *Encyclopedie* . . . was disorganized, so Charles Joseph . . . substituted an analytical for an alphabetical arrangement. Up in Uppsala, Linnaeus classified all the flora of the globe according to the System of Nature, and the Comte de Buffon added the rest of the natural world, man and animals, birds and fishes, and minerals for good measure. The indefatigable Antoine Reamur devoted six volumes to the classification of insects, while in Gottingen, Albrecht von Haller and Johann Blumenbach systemized the study of human anatomy" (2). Others, such as the Baron d'Holbach, or Montesquieu, or Bentham, tried to do the same for society and legal systems, just as Melvil Dewey and Charles Cutter were to do a century later for information. Everything was to be studied, investigated, classified, and organized in order to improve humans and society.

Political Enlightenment

The enduring legacy of the Enlightenment lives on in politics as much as in science, especially in the United States of America, which in some ways is the country best embodying Enlightenment principles in theory if not always in practice, and it was the first country founded upon ideas. Those ideas are easy to trace. We could meander through seventeenth and eighteenth century political philosophy for representative arguments that eventually built up to both the American and French Revolutions. We could explore Hobbes, Locke, Sidney, Montesquieu, Voltaire, Rousseau, Thomas Paine, or the English Commonwealthmen. However, for America it is easy enough to begin at the beginning, with the "Declaration of Independence."

We hold these truths to be self-evident, that all men are created equal, that they are endowed by their Creator with certain unalienable Rights, that among these are Life, Liberty and the pursuit of Happiness.--That to secure these rights, Governments are instituted among Men, deriving their just powers from the consent of the governed, --That whenever any Form of Government becomes destructive of these ends, it is the Right of the People to alter or to abolish it, and to institute new Government, laying its foundation on such principles and organizing its powers in such form, as to them shall seem most likely to effect their Safety and Happiness.

Key themes of Enlightenment political thought find forceful expression in this paragraph: individual liberty, equal rights, the sovereignty of the people and the consent of the governed, that the purpose of government is to secure liberty and order for its citizens, the belief that governments are not justified by tradition or divine revelation and can be changed if they abuse their citizens. These seem commonplace in America now, but they were radical ideas for the eighteenth century, just as they are still radical ideas for many around the world today. Rights enumerated in the United States Constitution and the Bill of Rights also reflect Enlightenment thought: freedom of the press, of religion, and of speech, the right to petition the government and to be free from arbitrary search and seizure. Even the checks and balances of the Constitution reflect a long line of thought from Aristotle's *Politics* to Montesquieu's *Spirit of the Laws* on the separation of powers and the best organization of a republic.

A similar document less well known in the United States, but that the historian Isaac Kramnik calls "a monumental summary of Enlightenment political thought," is the "Declaration of the Rights of Man and the Citizen," approved by the French National Assembly in 1789 (466). From Edmund Burke to Gertrude Himmelfarb, there has been a conservative tradition of criticizing even the motives of the French Revolution, not just its eventual course when the Revolution turned against its own Enlightenment principles. However, it is easy to see when examining the "Declaration of the Rights of Man and the Citizen" that the principles were no different from those motivating the American Revolution. We need only look at some relevant articles of the Declaration:

Humans have individual liberty and equal rights.

1. Men are born and remain free and equal in rights. Social distinctions may be founded only upon the general good.

Governments exist to secure those rights.

2. The aim of all political association is the preservation of the natural and imprescriptible rights of man. These rights are liberty, property, security, and resistance to oppression.

We are free to do whatever the law does not proscribe, rather than only what the law allows, a central tenet of a liberal society.

4. Liberty consists in the freedom to do everything which injures no one else; hence the exercise of the natural rights of each man has no limits except those which assure to the

other members of the society the enjoyment of the same rights. These limits can only be determined by law.

5. Law can only prohibit such actions as are hurtful to society. Nothing may be prevented which is not forbidden by law, and no one may be forced to do anything not provided for by law.

We are all equal before the law, and offices are available based on our virtues and talents, not on privileges and government favoritism.

6. Law is the expression of the general will. Every citizen has a right to participate personally, or through his representative, in its foundation. It must be the same for all, whether it protects or punishes. All citizens, being equal in the eyes of the law, are equally eligible to all dignities and to all public positions and occupations, according to their abilities, and without distinction except that of their virtues and talents.

Citizens cannot be arbitrarily arrested or imprisoned, but also no one is above the law.

7. No person shall be accused, arrested, or imprisoned except in the cases and according to the forms prescribed by law. Any one soliciting, transmitting, executing, or causing to be executed, any arbitrary order, shall be punished. But any citizen summoned or arrested in virtue of the law shall submit without delay, as resistance constitutes an offense.

We are free to express our opinions and beliefs, as long as we do not disrupt the public order.

10. No one shall be disquieted on account of his opinions, including his religious views, provided their manifestation does not disturb the public order established by law.

We are free to speak, write, and publish freely.

11. The free communication of ideas and opinions is one of the most precious of the rights of man. Every citizen may, accordingly, speak, write, and print with freedom, but shall be responsible for such abuses of this freedom as shall be defined by law.

Government agencies are accountable to the people.

15. Society has the right to require of every public agent an account of his administration.

Citizens have a right to private property.

17. Since property is an inviolable and sacred right, no one shall be deprived thereof except where public necessity, legally determined, shall clearly demand it, and then only on condition that the owner shall have been previously and equitably indemnified.

There is of course something missing from each of these documents, something that astute readers will no doubt already have noticed. First of all, we are told that all *men* are created equal. That is what the documents say, and that is what they meant. Second of all, neither document, nor the United States Constitution, abolishes slavery. With slavery, not even all men are treated equally.

The question for us now is whether the moral limitations of the eighteenth century are to be conflated with Enlightenment political theory, or whether it is the political theory of the Enlightenment that allows us to see the injustice of such inequality. Some critics of the Enlightenment take the strictly historicist route, even as they are claiming to evaluate Enlightenment thought for contemporary purposes. In her essay "The Gender of Enlightenment," the philosopher Robin May Schott includes an example of this kind of historicist claim (which she goes on to reject in her essay): "With many critics of the Enlightenment, I challenge its fundamental conception of rationality, autonomy, and freedom. This philosophical position has been the hallmark of a historical period in Western European and American society characterized by imperialism, the hegemony of dominant groups over other groups excluded from wealth, political power, and often basic human respect" (Schmidt 483). In other words, sexist, racist, imperialist slave traders may have espoused reason and freedom as political ideals, but because they were not able or willing to apply these ideals uniformly in their time, the ideals are somehow flawed.

Did slaveholders proclaim freedom a political ideal? Absolutely. Does it taint the ideals of Enlightenment? I would argue not. Such criticisms of the Enlightenment confuse history with philosophy, or perhaps refuse to recognize the difference because of the damage it does to their argument. Yes, the historical period known as the Enlightenment was also characterized by all sorts of activities now seen as evils by liberal thinkers: imperialism, slavery, inequality for women and other oppressed groups. Using this undeniable fact as a criticism of Enlightenment political thought is possible only because of equivocal meanings of Enlightenment — the historical and the philosophical. Certainly, Europeans and Americans during the eighteenth century committed brutal, and even despicable acts, but who can honestly claim that those Europeans and Americans were motivated by the thought of Spinoza, Locke, Voltaire, or Diderot? And just as certainly, Enlightenment thinkers themselves failed to apply their own values universally, and as such were limited by the practices of their time, but does this mean that the values themselves were linked to that failure? To make such claims is very problematic, but that is essentially the claim one has to make to support the conflation of Enlightenment philosophy with everything that happened during a historical period now knows as "the Enlightenment." If anything, it is the immanent critique within Enlightenment political thought that allows us to view the contrast between the rhetoric and practice of, say, Thomas Jefferson, as a contradiction.

Moving from the historical to the philosophical Enlightenment, we find more rigorous criticisms because of the variety of political thought emanating from the Enlightenment. For example, Spinoza wanted absolute toleration for all religious beliefs and expressions, while Locke's famous religious toleration was in fact limited to those members of various sects of the world's revealed religions (i.e., Judaism, Christianity, and Islam). Jonathan Israel argues in *Enlightenment Contested* that "Lockean toleration expressly denies liberty of thought to those who reject divine revelation and, still more, freedom of behavior to those who embrace a moral code divergent from that decreed for men by revelation" (139). Diderot wanted enlightenment for everyone, as his encyclopedia project implies, while Voltaire believed only the few should or could be enlightened. These differences exemplify the distinction

Israel makes between the Moderate Mainstream Enlightenment and the Radical Enlightenment. However, the Radical Enlightenment in support of individual liberty, political equality for *all* persons, and toleration of all non-violent religious practices clearly emerged as the dominant political thought in the West over the course of the past two hundred years, and is the standard against which we judge both other cultures and our own. This emergence gradually resolves the contradictions between Enlightenment ideals and the actual practice of people inspired by those ideals.

While it may also be true that Kant excluded women from the freedom and autonomy his political philosophy calls for (and there is little doubt that he does exclude women, as Schott and others amply demonstrate), that does not mean that the internal logic of his political philosophy excludes women, which is what some critics assume. That the men of the eighteenth century were not feminists can hardly be held against them when we view the matter *sub specie aeternitatis*, especially when we consider the anti-feminist views of many men around the world today.

These critics of the Enlightenment often, though not always, deliberately employ the most uncharitable hermeneutic possible to make their political points. Why not instead acknowledge, as many do, that only certain themes in Enlightenment thought allow us to view the exclusion of women or slaves from political freedom and equality as an injustice? Even arguments for the political equality of all men are recent in human history. If we see the belief in political equality in general and yet the toleration of inequality for women in the same thinker in the eighteenth century, it makes more sense to view the argument for equality as a fortunate liberal development from the dominant belief system rather than to believe that the novel arguments for political equality were somehow linked theoretically to arguments for inequality.

Such critics also seem to imply that they are the first to see the contradictions between the professions and actions of those living in the eighteenth century. If we conflate the historical and philosophical Enlightenments, then such a belief makes sense. If enlightened thought of the eighteenth century was equivalent to the actions of the majority of Europeans and Americans living during the historical period known as the Enlightenment, then of course only now that we are living not just in an age of enlightenment but an enlightened age can we see how foolish and contradictory these eighteenth-century folk were.

However, if we believe that the liberal and egalitarian claims of the Enlightenment were novel and separate from the actions of slave-traders, imperialists, and the like, then we would expect that the contradictions between enlightened thought and contemporary human action to be obvious even during the eighteenth century itself. This is exactly what we find. "The Declaration the Rights of Man and the Citizen" (1789) obviously excludes women from equal rights. We hardly had to wait for the enlightened twenty-first century to notice this glaring inconsistency. By 1791, Olympe de Gouges had published the "Declaration of the Rights of Woman and the Female Citizen." Her "Declaration" parallels that of the French National Assembly, but declaring rights for Woman, and not just Man. The opening is a stirring call for the true political equality demanded by Enlightenment ideals and the Revolution itself:

Man, are you capable of being just? It is a woman who poses the question; you will not deprive her of that right at least. Tell me, what gives you sovereign empire to oppress my sex? Your strength? Your talents? Observe the Creator in his wisdom; survey in all her grandeur that nature with whom you seem to want to be in harmony, and give me, if you dare, an example of this tyrannical empire. Go back to animals, consult the elements, study plants, finally glance at all the modifications of organic matter, and surrender to the evidence when I offer you the means; search, probe, and distinguish, if you can, the sexes in the administration of nature. Everywhere you will find them mingled; everywhere they cooperate in harmonious togetherness in this immortal masterpiece.

Man alone has raised his exceptional circumstances to a principle. Bizarre, blind, bloated with science and degenerated - in a century of enlightenment and wisdom - into the crassest ignorance, he wants to command as a despot a sex which is in full possession of its intellectual faculties; he pretends to enjoy the Revolution and to claim his rights to equality in order to say nothing more about it. (Kramnick 611)

Blind and degenerated into ignorance, even in a century of enlightenment and wisdom. De Gouges recognized then as clearly as any feminist today the contradictions between the rhetoric and actions of the revolutionaries. She could do so only if Enlightenment political ideas were to some extent separate from and more refined than eighteenth century practice. Fittingly enough, she also wrote an anti-slavery play. De Gouges was relentless in her criticisms of inequality, and for her pains was guillotined during the Reign of Terror.

Another thinker who must be considered impossibly prescient if we conflate the historical and philosophical Enlightenments is Mary Wollstonecraft, author of *A Vindication of the Rights of Men* (1790) and *A Vindication of the Rights of Woman* (1792). She wrote the first in response to Edmund Burke's reactionary *Reflections on the Revolution in France*, a lyrical if sometimes opaque defense of monarchy, aristocracy, established religion, and tradition. Wollstonecraft argued that rights are based not on tradition, but on reason and justice, perfectly in line with Enlightenment thought. She wrote the second vindication in response to a report on education to the French National Assembly, the *Rapport sur l'Instruction Publique, fait au nom du Comité de Constitution*, by Charles-Maurice de Talleyrand-Perigord, to whom she dedicated the work (Murray 1186). Talleyrand's *Rapport* called for unequal education for males and females in a national system of education on the grounds that men needed an education to operate in the public sphere, whereas women merely needed an education to perform domestic duties. Wollstonecraft, while not calling for the more widespread social equality that modern liberals would consider proper, forcefully argued that the so-called deficiencies men (and educated women like herself) found in so many women were not the result of nature, but of their lack of educational opportunities. That is, they are the effect of unequal education rather than the cause that justified it. Enlightenment political thought required the education of the people for the sustenance of liberty, and Wollstonecraft showed that women were people, too.

Undoubtedly, most persons in the eighteenth century, just like most persons today, could not live up to the challenge of the best and most enlightened thought of the day. Even revolutionaries devoted to political equality could ignore the oppression of women and slaves, but by doing so they acted in a contradictory manner, not out of enlightened motivations. Their historical blindness to their own contradictions hardly negates the universal appeal of enlightened political thought. Individual liberty, equal rights, religious toleration, freedom of speech, freedom of the press, the right to education and political participation in a democracy — these were core rights that emerged during the eighteenth century. Eighteenth-century thinking surged ahead of eighteenth-century practice, but the principles were in place. Contemporary calls for international human rights, or democracy in totalitarian states, or religious freedom in theocracies, all hearken back to the brave, bold, and sometimes inconsistent thinkers of the Enlightenment. Without them and all their mundane flaws, without the inspiring and incomplete examples of the "Declaration of Independence" or the "Declaration of the Rights of Man and the Citizen," we would have no United Nations' "Declaration of Human Rights" and no Amnesty International.

Some Contemporary Views of the Enlightenment

Criticisms of the Enlightenment are as old as the Enlightenment itself, though sometimes the criticisms evolve to meet new circumstances. What today passes for conventional wisdom in much of the West — such as the right to life, liberty, equal rights, and religious freedom — was as outrageous to the average seventeenth- or eighteenth-century European as it is to today's totalitarians or theocrats. In Iran, we hear of women being stoned to death for committing adultery or allegations "that a 26-year-old woman was raped and murdered by pro-government Basiji militiamen . . . after she was stopped for wearing clothes deemed not Islamic enough" (Iran). Few parts of Europe saw that level of violence against women in the eighteenth century, but criticisms of prevailing inequalities or established religions, and defenses of liberty, equality, and toleration (especially of the dreaded atheists!), could bring on vicious attacks and sometimes imprisonment. The same patterns of thought that inspired counter-Enlightenment forces in the eighteenth century still exist, and not just in Iran. Even in the United States today, there are groups who seek the establishment of a religious government and the repression of groups whose religious views differ from theirs. We have talk radio commentators who compare people who seek equal rights for women to Nazis, showing a massive ignorance of both feminism and Nazism. We have cults that keep their children away from schools and information and their followers locked behind walls. We have large pockets of Americans whose dedication to justice or racial equality is tepid or nonexistent. Many Americans, including those who have been victims of racial oppression, would happily deny equal rights to homosexuals. We have some conservatives inspired by Edmund Burke — the defender of aristocracy, monarchy, and established religion — still trying to criticize more radical elements of the Enlightenment because they go against Burke's exalted tradition.

And then we also have critiques of the Enlightenment from the left rather than from the right, such as that of Horkheimer and Adorno. Max Horkheimer's and Theodor Adorno's *Dialectic of Enlightenment: Philosophical Fragments* is considered by some a powerful critique of the Enlightenment. While there is insufficient space here for a full analysis of the *Dialectic of Enlightenment*, in general the book has only a marginal relationship to the Enlightenment as I have been discussing it. Horkheimer and Adorno are not really discussing "the Enlightenment," but instead a somewhat inchoate phenomenon emerging in various times and cultures from the ancient Greeks until today. "Enlightenment," as they discuss it, ranges from demythologization and disenchantment of the world — which occurs in ancient Greek as well as eighteenth century philosophy — to the reduction of humans and nature to abstract particles that are then manipulated as objects through purely instrumental reason. What starts out as enlightened critique undermines its own status, and as "Enlightenment" sinks into skepticism and myth, morality disappears into the sexual fantasies of the Marquis de Sade and the totalitarianism of the Nazis. Because if humans are released from their self-incurred tutelage, which Kant mentions as an example of enlightenment, then on their own they might choose the way of the Nazis, and "Enlightenment" would have nothing to say in return because it is concerned not with ends, but merely with means. The reduction of "Enlightenment" to instrumental rationality and abstraction, which then undermine Enlightenment itself, ignores considerable amounts of Enlightenment history and thought. Indeed, Homer, the Marquis de Sade, and Friedrich Nietzsche are amply represented in *Dialectic of Enlightenment*, but aside from Kant, almost no key figures of the European Enlightenment are mentioned, much less analyzed.

Even Kant's works that do not easily fit into their thesis are ignored. While they criticize Kant's version of Enlightenment thought, their target is a particular reading of his *Critique of Pure Reason*, while his moral philosophy is dismissed without analysis. They merely claim that "his attempt to derive the duty of mutual respect from a law of reason, although more cautious than any other such undertaking in Western philosophy, has no support within the *Critique*" (67). Or again, that fascism is a good example of the perils of Enlightenment rationality, because "contrary to the categorical imperative, and all the more deeply in accord with pure reason, it treats human beings as things, centers of modes of behavior." This lack of focused engagement with Kant might explain why Horkheimer and Adorno are usually absent figures in Kantian studies.

Though the work is chock full of interesting insights, in general it is long on analogy and short on analysis. For example, we are told that "the world as a gigantic analytical judgment, the only surviving dream of science is of the same kind as the cosmic myth which linked the alternation of spring and autumn to the abduction of Persephone" (20). That sort of grandiloquent rhetoric without supporting analysis and evidence is present throughout much of the work. In another anthropomorphic moment, we find not only that science has one surviving dream, but that "Reason's old ambition to be purely an instrument of purposes has finally been fulfilled" (23). They make much of the reductionism of modern science, but the claims are broad and usually lack specific examples.

While the danger of skepticism undermining claims of reason has always been present within philosophy, Horkheimer and Adorno make such claims while generally ignoring any evidence to the contrary. Consider the justly famous opening: "Enlightenment, understood in the widest sense as the advance of thought, has always aimed at liberating human beings from fear and installing them as masters. Yet the wholly enlightened earth is radiant with triumphant calamity" (1). At the time of writing during and after World War II, such gloomy pontificating from German exiles living comfortably in America might be forgiven, but as broad claims they lack specificity or support. The Nazis were responsible for the wholesale murder of millions of innocent people. Because of Adorno's and Horkheimer's peculiar reading of history, "Enlightenment" provides the motivation for this murder. The most devastating critique they offer of the United States is that the "culture industry" engages in mass deception of a gullible public, which is ironic considering that the Nazi culture industry did the same thing, but with truly evil consequences. Even compared to the treatment of African Americans at the time — a moral disgrace but hardly equivalent to the Holocaust — concern over the "culture industry" seems like small beer in a critique of failures of the Enlightenment in America. And compared to the horrors propagated by Nazi Germany, the American culture industry seems a benevolent distraction, not calamity triumphant. Although their chapter on the "culture industry" is among the most insightful and provocative of the book, in its forty-odd pages there are numerous grand claims, but almost no specific examples.

The work has some relevance to the German Enlightenment. Indeed, as we will see in Chapter II, several figures of the German Idealism movement influential in the history of higher education also rebelled against the pure instrumental rationality present in the German strain of the Enlightenment. However, regarding the Enlightenment outside Germany, either as an historical phenomenon or an ongoing project, *Dialectic of Enlightenment* is only marginally relevant. Its emphasis on Enlightenment as instrumental rationality while ignoring the long tradition of Enlightenment thinkers concerned with both reason *and* freedom means that their critique, though sometimes powerful, aims at something other than the Enlightenment thought that leads to the United Nations rather than the Holocaust.

Another influential critique of the Enlightenment comes from Michel Foucault. In a series of important works in the nineteen sixties and seventies — especially *History of Madness, The Birth of the Clinic, The Order of Things,* and *Discipline and Punish* — Foucault explored the dark side of the Enlightenment, the ways in which the desire to improve society through the use of reason led to systems of power controlling and sometimes repressing human beings. He gives a good, succinct summary of the legal aspects of this trend in *Discipline and Punish*:

> Historically, the process by which the bourgeoisie became in the course of the eighteenth century the politically dominant class was masked by the establishment of an explicit, coded and formally egalitarian juridical framework, made possible by the organization of a parliamentary, representative regime. But the development and generalization of disciplinary mechanisms constituted the other, dark side of these processes. The general juridical form that guaranteed a system of rights that were egalitarian in principle was supported by these tiny, everyday, physical mechanisms, by all those systems of micro-power that are essentially non-egalitarian and asymmetrical that we call the disciplines. . . . The 'Enlightenment', which discovered the liberties, also invented the disciplines. (222)

The disciplines control individuals within a society in many ways. For example, classifying certain behaviors as insane or criminal targets the individuals that behave in those ways. This might seem an obviously good thing to do, but classifications change over time. For example, the first edition of the American Psychiatric Association's *Diagnostic and Statistical Manual of Mental Disorders* listed homosexuality as a mental disorder, a classification that lasted until 1974. Thus, according to the leading psychiatric association in America, homosexuals were mentally ill and needed to be cured. A legal example might be the classification of marijuana alongside heroin as a Schedule I controlled substance by the United States' Controlled Substances Act. Schedule I includes drugs with "no accepted medical use," and the classification continues to receive challenges as the benefits of medical marijuana become more widely promoted. If marijuana were not illegal, prisons would be considerably less crowded. Classification always controls, which is why we use it, but it can also repress, which is why we must be careful.

While Horkheimer and Adorno write in broad generalities, Foucault focused on numerous concrete examples that showed the development of these disciplines, and because of that, it is difficult to evade his critique. The Enlightenment that discovered the liberties invented the disciplines. One might respond, so what? The development of psychiatry in the eighteenth century led to many problems, and was never a perfect example of the social or human improvement the Enlightenment might achieve. On the other hand, the treatment of the mentally ill — assuming for argument's sake that there are such people — was hardly better or more humane in previous eras. Likewise with prisons. The current prison-industrial complex contains many examples of injustice, but those examples are not necessarily examples of enlightened thinking (far from it), and while the panopticon Foucault discusses might metaphorically embody the worst aspects of the surveillance society, the treatment of prisoners was hardly better before the eighteenth century. Though some of his followers have gone further, Foucault usually acknowledged that we could not get past the influence of the Enlightenment, but should understand the complexities involved with power, liberty, and the disciplines. There is no story of perfect freedom without some unpleasant consequences emerging from Enlightenment thought.

It might seem that library science, though definitely one of the disciplines, is relatively free of their dark side, since the classification of information has less reach than the classification of mental illness or criminality. No one is arrested, imprisoned, or tortured because of cataloging rules. Nevertheless, as we can see in a work like Bowker and Star's *Sorting Things Out: Classification and its Consequences*, all classification schemes, even for information, have ethical and political ramifications, and we should strive to become aware of the values implicit in our classification schemes and the ways in which they might shape reality or disenfranchise library users. This might very well be the advice of the later Foucault regarding libraries.

Foucault's late address "What is Enlightenment?" interprets and evaluates Kant's own famous essay of that title. Here, he is critical of utopian thought, saying that "we know from experience that the claim to escape from the system of contemporary reality so as to produce the overall programs of another society, of another way of thinking, another culture, another vision of the world, has led only to the return of the most dangerous traditions," and that he prefers "even these partial transformations, which have been made in the correlation of historical analysis and the practical attitude, to the programs for a new man that the worst political systems have repeated throughout the twentieth century" (316). There can be no refutation or escape from modernity. Foucault offers his own interpretation of Enlightenment:

INTRODUCTION   31

> We know that the great promise or the great hope of the eighteenth century, or a part of the eighteenth century, lay in the simultaneous and proportional growth of individuals with respect to one another. And, moreover, we can see that throughout the entire history of Western societies . . . the acquisition of capabilities and the struggle for freedom have constituted permanent elements. Now, the relations between the growth of capabilities and the growth of autonomy are not as simple as the eighteenth century may have believed. And we have been able to see what forms of power relation were conveyed by various technologies: . . . disciplines, both collective and individual, procedures of normalization exercised in the name of the power of the state, demands of society or of population zones, are examples. What is at stake, then, is this: how can the growth of capabilities . . . be disconnected from the intensification of power relations? (317)

For Foucault, there is no wholesale escape from the influence of the Enlightenment, whether one is critical of the Enlightenment like Adorno or more celebratory of the Enlightenment such as Tzvetan Todorov. There is only a process of critique that we can apply to ourselves and our society to see if we can save the freedoms and capabilities discovered and developed during the Enlightenment while trying to escape the negative elements. Foucault's work could be considered a devastating criticism of repressive power relations stemming from the Enlightenment, or an exposure of social repression that enlightened critique still needs to address, including possible areas of social repression that emerge in relation to libraries.

Tzvetan Todorov's recent *In Defence of the Enlightenment* presents a more positive view of the influence of the Enlightenment, and argues that some criticisms more often react to *distortions* of Enlightenment thought than the thought itself. To understand his charge of distortion, we should examine how Todorov views the Enlightenment. "Three ideas are found at the basis of this project," he writes, "which produce countless consequences of their own: autonomy; the human end purpose of our acts; and universality" (5). We have already seen Kant privileging autonomy as a defining principle of Enlightenment. To the enlightened, for better or worse, we are on our own. Todorov divides the principle into two parts, emancipation and autonomy. We must be free from the demands of authority, and free to operate under rules decided by ourselves. Autonomy implies freedom of thought and expression as well. "To engage in it, one must have total freedom to examine, question, criticize and challenge dogmas and institutions: none can be regarded as sacred." In the West, it is difficult sometimes to understand the radical implications of such autonomy, because it has become so ingrained in our culture and consciousness. Before the eighteenth century in the West, and still today in much of the world, people lived under the constant pressure of religious and civil authorities directing their actions. Spoken beliefs about religion had to coincide with those of religious authorities if one wanted to avoid persecution. Contrast this with the contemporary West, where people choose their own religious beliefs or choose not to believe at all.

Certainly there are cultures within Western countries, including the United States, where forms of religious domination are practiced on children, and even where adults might feel that they are obligated to believe and act according to the religious beliefs of some authority. However, the adults *choose* their beliefs, even if they deny the choice, because outside of kidnapping and coercion, adults are free to leave religious communities if they so wish. Dissent, agnosticism, atheism, and free thought brought condemnation and persecution in Europe prior to the eighteenth century, which explains their rarity. In *The Courtier and the Heretic*, Matthew Stewart provides an excellent analogy in remarking that to appreciate Spinoza's boldness in publishing his quasi-atheistic views in the seventeenth century, "one would perhaps have to imagine a Jew propounding a skepticism such as his concerning the relevant sacred texts from within one of the modern world's existing theocracies — and then also imagine that there was no outside world in which he might seek asylum" (106). Our freedom to believe what we like and act how we like — as long as we harm no one — is precious and rare in human history, and the result of bold thinkers of the Enlightenment sometimes risking their lives or liberty to develop their philosophy of freedom and autonomy.

Emancipation and autonomy are not merely negative. They lead to creative activity and imply a host of positive values. For example, as Todorov notes, "the emancipation of knowledge paved the way for the development of science" (7). Critics of the Enlightenment and of modern science might bemoan the horrors that science and the quest to understand and use nature has allegedly brought us, but these critics almost always choose to criticize from within the relatively safe, comfortable, healthy countries influenced by the Enlightenment. The mistake is thinking that science itself is the problem, rather than human limitations. The scientific spirit drives us to know, because autonomous human beings require knowledge. Because we require knowledge, we also require education, especially if we are to develop into worthwhile citizens of democratic republics. Because we require not only education but broad and continuous access to information, autonomy also implies that we must have the freedom to speak and publish freely, and test our ideas against arguments and facts without fear of persecution from a repressive state or church. How we apply this knowledge once we have it is not a scientific question, though, but an ethical one.

The individual freedom our autonomy demands for ourselves is not boundless, as some counter-Enlightenment critics have charged. It also demands that we respect the right of others to the same level of freedom. We have the right to speak freely, but we do not have the right *not* to be offended. We have the right to practice or not practice religion, but we also must tolerate the non-violent religious practices of others. The enlightened state exists not to coerce or oppress or dispense privileges to the favored few, but to enforce this liberal toleration of difference and to promote the welfare of all its citizens. Natural human rights, popular sovereignty, the separation of church and state, the checks and balances of government — all these stem from the principle of human autonomy, which, because of the universality of its demands, restrains even as it emancipates. Liberty does not mean just doing anything you want, as John Locke argued in his *Two Treatises on Government* when discussing the "state of nature." "But though this be a state of liberty," Locke writes, "yet it is not a state of licence. . . . The state of nature has a law of nature to govern it, which obliges every one: and reason, which is that law, teaches all mankind, who will but consult it, that being all equal and independent, no one ought to harm another in his life, health, liberty, or possessions" (Kramnick 396). Proponents of the Enlightenment project usually accept something like this vision of the Enlightenment, with all its warts and problems. Often enough, critics of Enlightenment do as well, and from certain perspectives there is much to criticize. Devout religious believers who also believe that everyone should worship as they do understandably dislike or even fear freedom and autonomy. Despots and demagogues of all political persuasions do as well.

Sometimes, though, critics attack something they claim to be the Enlightenment or inspired by the Enlightenment project. Todorov takes on some of these distortions. A common conservative criticism claims that Enlightenment thought foolishly believed in the perfectibility of human beings. Certainly there were many Enlightenment thinkers who believed that reason and education would help humans improve their lot. This belief is so common in the West today that to deny it would seem like madness, so some conservatives (Russell Kirk comes to mind) attribute to Enlightenment thinkers the belief that humans could be perfected, and then criticize that straw man. William Godwin is sometimes a target of this criticism, and indeed he believed in human perfectibility. However, an examination of his *Enquiry Concerning Political Justice and its Influence on Morals and Happiness* shows that by that he did not mean that humans are "capable of being brought to perfection," but instead have the "faculty of being continually made better and receiving perpetual improvement," which he argues is opposed to the idea of perfection, for "if we could arrive at perfection, there would be an end of our improvement" (Godwin 89). Perfectibility is a process, perfection a status, and the possibility of the former does not imply the possible attainment of the latter.

The notion of perfectibility through Enlightenment implies a belief in human progress. Todorov shows that many leading thinkers — Voltaire, Turgot, Condorcet — did believe that over time humans "would eventually reach adulthood through the spread of culture and knowledge" (18). That humans individually and socially are capable of progress — technological, political, and ethical — is almost indisputable, but that does not mean that such progress is either easy or inevitable. We also see that many other thinkers — Hume and Rousseau, for example — disputed any guaranteed human progress. Todorov argues that the belief in inevitable human progress was taken up by Hegel and then Marx where it became standard communist doctrine. The standard communist narrative of salvation had History marching inevitably toward the perfection of humanity through communism. Unfortunately for those on the wrong (i.e., liberal, non-communist) side of History, the inevitability of the communist triumph meant that anyone opposed to that triumph could or should be eliminated to make way for the communist paradise. Thus, the logic of perfectibility and the inevitability of progress can indeed be turned into a weapon of oppression and political murder. However, this has little to do with the Enlightenment. Communism, according to Todorov, claimed the heritage of the Enlightenment without living it. In communist societies, "individual autonomy was reduced to nothing, the principle of equality was belied by the omnipresence of unchanging hierarchies within the governing class, the search for knowledge was subjected to ideological dogmas, . . . and the 'humanism' of the manifestos was but a mirage" (35). Despite the lack of guaranteed progress, however, I think most would agree that Americans and most Europeans are better off both technologically and politically than the subjects of pre-Enlightenment European states or the people in many areas of the world where the Enlightenment had no effect.

Liberty, democracy, equality, freedom of thought and expression: the list of Enlightenment values eliminated under communism or fascism is so extensive that to claim communism or fascism are somehow the result of the Enlightenment implies an extremely misguided criticism. Earlier, we saw that some critics conflate or even confuse the historical and philosophical to make their criticisms stick. We have also seen that some critics distort their picture of the Enlightenment. A third and related mistake is selective criticism that chooses values in isolation, whether distorting them in the process or not, and then criticizes those values or the ends to which they have allegedly led. However, the values of the Enlightenment comprise a system; they are interrelated in important ways, as we have seen from the list of political values implied by the concept of autonomy. The use of human reason to improve the practical lot of humanity is indeed an Enlightenment value; the use of instrumental rationality alone to solve technical problems such as how to most efficiently kill the largest numbers of Jews is not. The belief that more education, knowledge, freedom, and equality will lead to human progress is an Enlightenment belief; that every brutal and murderous act aiming towards communism is morally justifiable because progress in a certain direction is inevitable is not.

While counter-Enlightenment critics from the left and right sometimes base their criticisms on one or another mistaken approach, many operating within the Enlightenment tradition proceed just as myopically. The Enlightenment considered reason and skepticism as crucial values alongside liberty or equality, but even passionate defenders of liberty sometimes misuse their reason or suppress their skepticism. A good historical example of this came to be known as "Whig history," a phrase coined by the British historian Herbert Butterfield in his 1931 *The Whig Interpretation of History*. Butterfield criticized previous generations of historians for studying the past as if it was an inevitable progression toward the alleged perfection of the British parliamentary, constitutional monarchy. "Whig history" has broadened in meaning to include any historical interpretation that sees the past as merely prologue to the inevitable rise of enlightened societies governed by liberal democracy and dedicated to scientific progress. The assumption is that the way we are now is the apex of human history, and that such perfection came about because of the inevitable increase of enlightenment. In Francis Fukuyama's 1992 *The End of History and the Last Man*, a variation of Whig history makes an appearance, since Fukuyama argued that the triumph of liberal democracy after the Cold War marks "the end of history as such: that is, the end point of mankind's ideological evolution and the universalization of Western liberal democracy as the final form of human government" (4). Fukuyama's initial argument has received a good deal of criticism, and from an Enlightenment perspective the suggestion is obviously problematic. If by "Western liberal democracy" we mean the sort of states enlightened political thinkers would desire, or even if we mean just the best versions of these states that have been put into practice, such states are far from universalized (as, to be fair, Fukuyama well knows). If we gaze out at the world from an American or Western perspective it may seem that our civilization is triumphant, the same forces of darkness and oppression that existed in eighteenth-century Europe still exist in strong or mild forms in every country, including our own.

Because every subject is open to investigation and challenge, we can focus our attention not just on the obviously brutal, unjust, oppressive regimes and cultures around the world, but also on our own relatively enlightened one. I make this statement knowing that there are Americans on the left and right who seem to believe the United States of America (or even AmeriKKKa) is somehow the most evil nation on earth, whether because of its imperialism, its arrogance, or its estrangement from (or manifestation of) Christian values. Such complete and assured beliefs about any country are always based on loose reasoning and selective blindness. We criticize our country often enough not because it compares unfavorably with much of the world, but because it compares unfavorably to the Enlightenment ideal implicit in its founding. One of the dangers of an unskeptical and unenlightened patriotism is to believe that because our country is founded on high ideals, everything the current government does must also be motivated by those ideals, or that every citizen of the country actually believes in or is motivated by those ideals. Within America and at times within the American government itself there are those who peel away values from the Enlightenment system and use those isolated values to promote unenlightened ends. "Freedom" and "democracy" are the values most likely to be isolated and abused, and they have always been problematic values to invoke to support American interests abroad. In "Taxation No Tyranny," his hostile response to American calls for "liberty" from the British government, Samuel Johnson asked, "How is it that we hear the loudest yelps for liberty among the drivers of negroes?" (454). Because of the American tendency for high-minded rhetoric, even when it is not accompanied by aggressive invasions of foreign countries and the torture of prisoners in the name of "freedom," patriots themselves should be the most cautious about the claims of their government, as we are reminded in another famous saying of Dr. Johnson that "patriotism is the last refuge of a scoundrel."

Let us conclude this brief survey of the Enlightenment with the work of the historian Jonathan Israel. For the past decade or so, Israel has been revising the intellectual history of the Enlightenment. Up through the nineteen sixties, culminating with Peter Gay's two-volume history of the Enlightenment, scholars tended to view the Enlightenment as somehow unified, whether they were hostile critics such as Adorno and Horkheimer or sympathetic admirers like Ernst Cassirer or Peter Gay. The consensus shifted in the nineteen seventies with the rise of microhistory and "history from below." For a couple of decades historians of the Enlightenment tended toward disintegration and to some extent a de-intellectualizing of the Enlightenment. In this context, it makes much more sense to talk of Enlightenments than *the* Enlightenment, because historians complicated the previous view of Enlightenment and the eighteenth century. Now we distinguish between national Enlightenments, for example, understanding that whatever passes for Enlightenment differed in Britain, France, Germany, Poland, America, or whatever country one chooses to focus upon. Ideas as motivating factors became less interesting or important than other social relations. Robert Darnton's work provides us with good examples of this trend. In his *The Business of Enlightenment*, he focuses on the nuts and bolts of publication in eighteenth century France, and shows incontestably that most people did not care about enlightenment, and that most people did not read the famous or infamous books of the age, and that instead those who could read preferred slighter and shallower popular works that entertained rather than challenged them. In other words, most people in eighteenth century France were like most people today.

Israel writes in reaction to this trend, not to repudiate the findings, but to bring the power of ideas back into intellectual history. In two massive and wide-ranging volumes — *Radical Enlightenment: Philosophy and the Making of Modernity, 1650-1750* and *Enlightenment Contested: Philosophy, Modernity, and the Emancipation of Man 1670-1752* — he teases out not one, but two strands of Enlightenment political thought, which he terms the Moderate Mainstream Enlightenment and the Radical Enlightenment. The Moderate Mainstream Enlightenment is the enlightenment of Locke or Voltaire — it challenges many traditional ideas and provides the beginning of newer and more modern ways of viewing the world, but it is still bound by traditional political and religious loyalties that would seem out of place in contemporary secular liberal democracies. The Radical Enlightenment, by contrast, begins with the work of Israel's intellectual hero Spinoza, who, Israel argues, for the first time in human history makes the case for the secular, liberal, egalitarian, humanistic, democratic republicanism that characterizes countries in the modern West.

Rather than provide any in-depth analysis of his exhaustive works, I will provide Israel's own summary of the Radical Enlightenment from his shorter and more accessible *Revolution of the Mind: Radical Enlightenment and the Intellectual Origins of Modern Democracy*:

> Radical Enlightenment is a set of basic principles that can be summed up concisely as: democracy; racial and sexual equality;

> individual liberty of lifestyle; full freedom of thought, expression, and the press; eradication of religious authority from the legislative process and education; and full separation of church and state. It sees the purpose of the state as being the wholly secular one of promoting the worldly interests of the majority and preventing vested minority interests from capturing control of the legislative process. Its chief maxim is that all men have the same basic needs, rights, and status irrespective of what they believe or what religious, economic, or ethnic group they belong to, and that consequently all ought to be treated alike, on the basis of equity, whether black or white, male or female, religious or nonreligious, and that all deserve to have their personal interests and aspirations equally respected by law and government. Its universalism lies it its claim that all men have the same right to pursue happiness in their own way, and think and say whatever they see fit, and no one, including those who convince others they are divinely chosen to be their masters, rulers, or spiritual guides, is justified in denying or hindering others in the enjoyment of rights that pertain to all men and women equally. (vi-vii)

As should be clear, by Radical Enlightenment Israel means more or less those political beliefs developed during the seventeenth and eighteenth centuries that eventually triumphed over the more conservative beliefs in divine-right monarchies or established churches or "enlightened despots" as the foundation for liberal democracies in the West. As he describes it,

> Radical Enlightenment is the system of ideas that, historically, has principally shaped the Western World's most basic social and cultural values in the post-Christian age. This in

itself lends the history of the movement great importance. But this type of thought — especially in many Asian and African countries, as well as in contemporary Russia — has also become the chief hope and inspiration of numerous besieged and harassed humanists, egalitarians, and defenders of human rights, who, often against great odds, heroically champion basic human freedom and dignity, including that of women, minorities, homosexuals, and religious apostates, in the face of the resurgent forms of bigotry, oppression, and prejudice that in much of the world today appear inexorably to be extending their grip. (xi)

We end with this vision of Enlightenment. Eighteenth-century Europe and America present us with complicated histories, even if we restrict ourselves merely to intellectual history. For every proponent of Enlightenment, there were hundreds of detractors; for every radical idea, thousands of reactionary ones.

If we consider the Enlightenment as a period of history, we must along with Darnton and many others continue to see it as more complex and more quotidian than if we consider the Enlightenment to be a living intellectual tradition, an Enlightenment project. Israel's work reinforces this view of Enlightenment. He digs deeply into the intellectual history of the period and discloses raging debates over socinianism or materialism that now seem trivial or obscure, but that helped form the modern consciousness. However, he is certainly not writing Whig history, because it is clear that while a system of ideas emerged as the foundations of Enlightenment, Enlightenment has yet to fully triumph.

Philosophical and Political Enlightenment and Libraries

What, one may now understandably ask, does all this have to do with libraries? My own inspiration to write on this topic was Israel's book *Radical Enlightenment*, specifically the chapter on "Libraries and Enlightenment," which was my first introduction to the thought of Gabriel Naudé, a seventeenth-century librarian who wrote the first treatise on the development of a research library, and whom I discuss in Chapter IV. From the very beginning of libraries, libraries and politics have always been intertwined. The earliest libraries were royal libraries, designed to hold the secular and sacred knowledge kings needed to rule over their people. Libraries and politics are still inseparable, and what we might call the American library project is a development of the Enlightenment project, including both its philosophical and political values. In the rest of the book, I hope to make clear how the principles of Enlightenment outlined here provide the philosophical foundation for American academic and public libraries. And just as the Enlightenment project has yet to triumph as the end of history, it has also yet to triumph in contemporary libraries.

In what follows, I will be using my own division of Enlightenment principles to organize this survey of library history. We can very roughly divide the Enlightenment into the philosophical and the political. By Philosophical Enlightenment, I mean all those principles of Enlightenment that coalesce around scholarship and research, the increase of knowledge, the belief in the benefits of science and education, and the right and even obligation to publish scholarly findings. The Philosophical Enlightenment shares something with the Moderate Mainstream Enlightenment in that while it is undoubtedly Enlightenment, it is not Enlightenment for everyone. In contrast, Political Enlightenment could be considered the Philosophical Enlightenment democratized — Enlightenment at least within the reach of everyone, even if not desired by everyone.

This rough division plays itself out in the history of libraries. Academic libraries — and the universities they support — to a great extent fulfill the promises of the Philosophical Enlightenment to collect, organize, preserve, and within limitations disseminate scholarly knowledge and the human record. Public libraries fall into the category of the Political Enlightenment, and many have conceived their mission partly as one of making knowledge (or information) more available to people. Enlightenment — philosophical and political — involves the creation of knowledge and its democratic dissemination to prepare autonomous citizens of a democratic republic, as well as the improvement of their lives in various ways. Libraries have always formed an important pillar of the Enlightenment project, and they continue to do so today. As I hope to show, without Enlightenment there might still be libraries, but without libraries there can be no Enlightenment.

CHAPTER II

Academic Libraries *and the* Philosophical Enlightenment

A CADEMIC LIBRARIES ARE inherently related to the institutions they support, so a history of their development is also a history of the development of higher education. While universities have existed in Europe from about the eleventh century, the modern research university as we know it is of relatively recent origin, as is the system of academic libraries supporting modern research universities. Its creation was directly inspired by thinkers of the German Enlightenment. Kant, from whom we heard earlier, and his fellow German Idealists Fichte, Schelling, Schiller, Schleiermacher, and others developed the foundational ideas of modern research universities that still generally hold today. The result of their thinking and planning, the University of Berlin (founded 1810), was the first true research university in the world. It in turn inspired the pattern known as the German Model, or sometimes the Humboldtian Model. The German Model was imported piecemeal into the United States during the mid-nineteenth century and provided the pattern for the first university in the United States dedicated completely to research — The Johns Hopkins University, founded in 1876. Prompted by the success of Johns Hopkins, Cornell, and other universities, the German Model became over the next fifty years the model that most large American universities sought to emulate, and the values of those universities trickled down even into smaller four-year colleges. The devotion to knowledge for its own sake and untrammeled research into every domain of knowledge was made possible by the growth and development of academic libraries from the small reading rooms of the nineteenth century into the enormous research libraries we have today. The organization of information and networks of information sharing that librarians have developed over the last 135 years or so have created almost a *de facto* universal library for scholars at American colleges and universities. The vast system of American higher education and the even more integrated system of academic libraries are products of the Enlightenment, and the end result of a few eighteenth century German philosophers working out their ideas of reason, knowledge, and freedom.

The Enlightenment and German Idealism

Over time, enlightened ideas spread through much of Western Europe, though at different paces. Germany experienced its own Enlightenment toward the end of the eighteenth century, and we saw earlier Immanuel Kant's contribution to the raging debate over just what *"Aufklärung"* was supposed to mean. For Kant and others, Enlightenment meant that people should think for themselves rather than irrationally following traditions or authority. We can see even today how difficult this standard is for people to achieve, especially those raised in traditionalist countries or cultures. We might now say *conservative* countries or cultures, because conservatism as a word and later a movement itself began as a reaction to the Enlightenment promotion of human reason and freedom, with some of the most reactionary voices — such as that of Joseph de Maistre — coming from France, the country often considered the heart of the Enlightenment. The clash between Enlightenment and the reaction against it certainly affected Germany. For example, Kant's essay "What is Enlightenment?" was published in 1784, near the end of the reign of Frederick the Great of Prussia, whose commitment to enlightened absolutism gave Kant and other academics some freedom of teaching and publication. This freedom grew strained after Frederick's death in 1786, when the throne went to his very conservative nephew, Friedrich Wilhelm II. Religiously and politically, Germany was undergoing the turmoil that always attends the clash between Enlightenment values and traditionalist cultures.

This turmoil emerged in intellectual debates as the Enlightenment spread throughout German philosophical circles, leading to the development of the movement known as German Idealism. The foundation of the crisis was the clash between reason and tradition, and this can be formulated in various ways. For example, Frederick Beiser argues that the crisis was a reaction to the "dire" consequences of the "fundamental principles of the Enlightenment," which "were rational criticism and scientific naturalism. While criticism seemed to end in skepticism, naturalism appeared to result in materialism. Both results were unacceptable" (18). That the results were "unacceptable," of course, does not mean they were mistaken, but that they clashed with traditional values that the thinkers wanted to keep. Materialism, for example, was unacceptable not because it could be refuted by reason and evidence, but because it left no room outside of nature for such notions as God or the human soul, which were ideas that had to be kept regardless of the evidence. This debate still rages, usually as a "war" between science and religion.

Reason and skepticism have always created conflicts for philosophers, with particularly strong strains of skepticism emerging in ancient Greece and Rome and again in Renaissance Europe. During the eighteenth century, rationalist criticism had led to a radical skepticism in some thinkers, notably David Hume, whose skeptical undermining of metaphysics and such notions as cause and effect led Kant to develop his own defense of reason. Kant was particularly critical of some philosophical movements within the Scottish Enlightenment that dealt with the problem of Hume's skepticism through "common sense." In his *Prolegomena to any Future Metaphysics*, he argued that common sense was a "great gift of heaven," but that it "must be shown in deeds by well-considered and reasonable thoughts and words, not by appealing to it as an oracle when no rational justification of oneself can be advanced" (5). According to Will Dudley, "modernity calls for a re-evaluation of our ordinary beliefs and practices that brings them into accord with the demands of reason, but Hume's denial of the very possibility of this enterprise gives rise to the need for a critical examination of rationality itself." Thus, it is the task of philosophy to show "that Hume fails to establish that reason is incapable of directing and motivating human behavior, and thus fails to establish that human beings are not free" (10). In the *Prolegomena*, Kant wrote that Hume's philosophy awoke him from his "dogmatic slumber" (5). The end of that dogmatic slumber was the beginning of the German Idealist movement, the goal of which Beiser argues was to "to preserve the legacy of the Enlightenment" (19). Within the context of "the Enlightenment insistence on replacing the premodern acceptance of unjustified authority with the modern demand for rational justification and freedom," as Will Dudley puts it, "German Idealism is best understood as the philosophical manifestation of the modern demand for rationality and freedom" and "grew out of Kant's attempt to defeat the threat posed to this demand by Hume's scepticism and determinism" (2). The movement encompassed many German thinkers influenced by Kant — including Johann Gottlieb Fichte, Friedrich Schleiermacher, and Friedrich Schelling — who were important in the creation of the first research university. Their philosophical attempts to respond to both radical skepticism and to Kant's own response to that skepticism "led them to different conclusions about what it means to be rational and free" (183), but nevertheless rationality and freedom developed from Enlightenment thought to spur a profound rethinking of higher education and its purposes.

German Idealism and Higher Education

To see how the Enlightenment values of reason and freedom manifested themselves in higher education, we should consider the thought of the German Idealists on higher education and their influence on the founding of the University of Berlin. Unlike Enlightenment thinkers in France or England — who tended to be amateur philosophers while often making their living in some other way — the Enlightenment in Germany was very much an academic affair. Kant, Fichte, Schleiermacher, and Schelling, for example, were all professors, and their thinking led to a renewal of higher education in Germany and via the German Model the United States.

For those familiar with modern universities as they have been in America for a century, where scholars are expected to produce original research on every conceivable topic, it might be difficult to understand just how new this model of higher education actually is. Universities, or at least bodies calling themselves universities, existed prior to the eighteenth century, but they were usually institutions specializing in training future lawyers, doctors, and theologians, not in producing scholarship as such. The faculties of law, medicine, and theology were the most powerful in most universities, whereas the faculty of philosophy (the group we now associate with the liberal arts and sciences) was the weakest faculty, and almost always confined to undergraduate education. Moreover, universities or the colleges sometimes comprising them were dedicated to transmitting received knowledge rather than in producing new knowledge. Universities were there to pass on existing knowledge and train professionals in circumscribed disciplines.

American colleges rarely included professional schools until the mid-nineteenth century or so, but the dedication to passing on received knowledge especially in religion and the classics, often through recitation, persisted at most American colleges well into the nineteenth century. Such institutions did not need large libraries. So what changed all that? The change came about partly because of the influence of Enlightenment thought on German professors struggling to conceive of institutions of higher education dedicated to reason, liberty, and the pursuit of truth and knowledge for its own sake. As Daniel Fallon puts it in his book on the German university, "perhaps the most remarkable fact about the widely admired German university of the nineteenth century is that it had no clear precedent. The university idea was struck, virtually *de novo*, by scholars and aristocrats of the enlightenment from only a few fleeting practical examples and with only a passing glance at history" (5). Though universities were old, *this* idea of the university was very new.

One note before we examine the German Idealists on higher education. It is important to distinguish "philosophy" and "science" as they were meant in the eighteenth century from the meanings they sometimes have today. In particular, science, or what the Germans call *Wissenschaft*, then did not mean just the natural sciences, as English speakers tend to assume today; instead it meant any organized body of knowledge pursued more or less objectively with standards of reason and evidence guiding progress. Thus, one could study religion "scientifically," and in fact it was the scientific study of the Bible by German scholars that revolutionized modern textual criticism. Instead of scientists, English speakers in the eighteenth century would have had "natural philosophers," and philosophy itself was as inclusive as science. Thus, when Kant or Schleiermacher speak of philosophy or science, they do not necessarily mean the academic fields of philosophy or the natural sciences that we do, but instead meant those fields where knowledge and truth were pursued for their own sake.

So let us consider Kant's thoughts on universities in his *Conflict of the Faculties*, written near the end of his life to defend the freedom of the "lower" philosophy faculty against the predations of the "higher" faculties of theology, law, and medicine. According to Kant, the higher faculties are utilitarian in nature; that is, they instruct on the current situation of practical fields, but do not pursue knowledge for its own sake. The philosophy faculty is the only faculty concerned with truth as such, with "teachings which are not adopted as directives by order of a superior." We may accept such teachings because we are ordered to, but this has nothing to do with truth. Questions of truth cannot be settled by force, but only by reason, which is the "power to judge autonomously" and freely "according to the principles of thought in general." Thus, because the philosophy faculty "must answer for the truth of the teachings it is to adopt or even allow," it "must be conceived as free and subject only to laws given by reason, not by the government" (43). This is a bold claim to make in an authoritarian state that funded all of the universities, but a claim easily traced to Kant's thought about what Enlightenment is.

The necessity for the independence of science from political and religious control pervades the thoughts of the German Idealists on higher education. Kant argued that one purpose of the philosophy faculty was to test the claims of the state and the faculties of theology, law, and medicine against a standard of truth, which of course annoys the higher faculties because then they cannot "rest undisturbed in possession of what they have once occupied, but whatever title, and rule over it despotically" (45). The higher faculties resist the rational criticisms of the philosophy faculty, and attempt to "illegally" suppress them. The philosophical faculty must resist this suppression, and even the wrath of "the people," who prefer to avoid the hard standards of philosophy. The people, Kant says, want security and physical enjoyment in life and happiness after death. Philosophers argue with reason that such goals are met by living righteously and moderately, but people want easier answers from the higher faculties. Kant imagines the thoughts of people seeking easy answers:

> As for the *philosophers'* twaddle, I've known that all along. What I want you, as men of learning, to tell me is this: if I've been a *scoundrel* all my life, how can I get an eleventh-hour ticket to heaven? If I've *broken* the law, how can I still win my case? And even if I've used and *abused* my physical powers as I've pleased, how can I stay healthy and live a long time? (49)

How indeed, many still ask. Perhaps a fad diet or a self-help guru can help. Kant's point is that the answers to those questions should be tested by the use of reason, not by the claims of an authority that from the standpoint of reason is completely arbitrary.

Friedrich Schleiermacher makes much the same point in his *Occasional Thoughts on Universities in the German Sense*. Schleiermacher, according to Terrence Tice in the introduction to his translation of *Occasional Thoughts*, "crafted and most eminently sustained [the] vision that in large part underlay the University [of Berlin]'s design" (ii). Schleiermacher considers it a "pernicious misunderstanding" of the purpose of universities to allow political considerations to outweigh scientific ones. Allowing politics to trump the search for truth stifles "the highest and freest culture and all scientific spirit; and the unfailing result in all departments is that a mechanistic way of being and a deplorable narrow-mindedness get the upper hand" (26). He considers religious or political institutes affiliated with universities as Kant considered the higher faculties, as groups that "must declare themselves dependent on and must subsist on the scientific treatment of the nature and history, and along with that, on philosophy" (28). As with Kant, the ultimate purpose of a university — the pursuit of truth and knowledge for their own sake — lay with the philosophical faculty.

In *On University Studies*, Friedrich Schelling reinforces this point. He assumes that it is in the interest of the state to create genuinely scientific institutions, for otherwise the university's goal to further knowledge is undermined. For Schelling, authority rests in reason, not in arbitrary power. Not even professors deserve respect because of their titles alone, for "no teacher worthy of his vocation will demand respect on any other grounds than the superiority of his intelligence, the breadth of his learning, and the zeal with which he seeks to communicate them" (22). Admittedly, he says, "the state has the authority to suppress the universities or to transform them into industrial training schools; however, it cannot intend the universities to be real scientific institutions without desiring to further the life of ideas and the freest scientific development" (23). This is at a time when university professorships might be handed out as patronage, or avenues of study restricted because the results of investigation conflict with religious doctrine or political sensibilities. Science, or the pursuit of knowledge, must be allowed to go where it will, and it cannot develop otherwise, for "science ceases to be science the moment it is degraded to a *mere* means, rather than furthered for its own sake" (23, note 6).

Johann Gottlieb Fichte, perhaps the German Idealist philosopher with the most ambition for higher education, concurs, and for much the same reason. In order for society to progress, science must progress — and remember he means science as knowledge in the widest sense — and science cannot progress unless scholars are free to pursue their investigations wherever they might lead. If any areas of investigation are restricted because of religious or political reasons, then all areas of investigation suffer. Much as Kant imagined the voice of another opponent of science, the people, Fichte imagines the voice of those who would impede the free progress of science and knowledge.

> As long as *I* live, the people around me shall not become better and wiser, for their vigorous progress would carry forth even me, in spite of all my resistance! That I would detest. I don't want to be enlightened, I don't want to become more noble: darkness and perversion are my elements, and I will make every effort to be removed from them. Humanity can do without everything, can be robbed of everything, without losing its dignity — except the possibility of self improvement. (55)

Fichte considered it the purpose of everyone, but particularly the scholar, to aim for the "moral enoblement of the entire human being" (59), and this enoblement is impossible if the enemies of reason and enlightenment are allowed to control universities.

In one of his plays, the ancient Roman playwright Terrence wrote, "I am a man. Nothing human to is alien to me." The same could be said of the philosophical founders of the modern university. The purpose of a university is to pursue knowledge in all areas for its own sake, which requires the faculty to be free to investigate as they will. In the *Conflict of the Faculties*, Kant claims that the intellectual domain of the philosophy faculty "extends to all parts of human knowledge (including, from a historical viewpoint, the teachings of the higher faculties)," which means the philosophy faculty can "lay claim to any teaching, in order to test its truth" (45).

Fichte considered scientific knowledge a "part of human culture," and argued that "each branch of it must be developed, if the capacities of humanity are to be developed." Thus, every scholar "has the right . . . to further scientific knowledge, and particularly the discipline that he or she has chosen for himself or herself" (55). Schelling insisted that the "purpose for which [universities] were founded" is "the furthering of knowledge" (28). For Schleiermacher, "the university thus has to embrace all knowing" (16), and "the true spirit of the university is that of allowing the greatest freedom possible to prevail within every faculty as well" (39). The intellectual domain of the scholar, and thus of the university, was boundless. Every area of knowledge was now considered open for investigation, and the scholar free to follow the investigation wherever it lead.

Two principles especially articulated the freedom of the scholar: the freedom to learn (*lernfreiheit*) and the freedom to teach (*lehrfreiheit*). Both were crucial for universities to function effectively in their search for knowledge. Ideally, a university would not be like a school. Schools are designed to transmit the current state of knowledge to their students, who are relatively passive learners. In universities, students are also fellow scholars who are also doing original research, even if only as novices. They are learning to be scholars themselves. The university is to awaken the spirit of scientific investigation in students who then go on to master a field of study. They learn how to learn. As Schleiermacher puts it, "only one moment is actually spent at the university, only one act is completed; the idea of knowledge, the highest consciousness of reason, awakens in the person as a regulative principle" (17). Schleiermacher considered student freedom almost unlimited, arguing that students should not be "subject to compulsion of any kind; never will they be forced in any direction, and nothing is closed to them. No one orders them to attend this or that course session; no one can reproach them if they neglect or omit to do their work" (50). Students should be free to learn what they like, and free to fail if they choose not to work. If the idea of students learning to be scholars and having unlimited freedom seems odd, you should consider American graduate students in the liberal arts and sciences to be the closest parallel to the students Schleiermacher is referring to, which explains why the impetus to create research universities in the United States centered on the creation of graduate schools that were usually grafted onto already existing colleges. Graduate students are free from any attempt by universities to act *in loco parentis*. Nevertheless, Schleiermacher's support of almost unlimited student freedom was still remarkable in an era when student freedom might end in drunken undergraduate duels, a practice that makes current undergraduate practice seem almost tame in comparison.

So the ideal university was to be a place where scholars were free to study any field whatever, and their investigations were free to go wherever reason led them. The scholars were to specialize in their research and delve deeply into their subjects, for otherwise they would be unable to teach their subjects well; thus, research and teaching must be unified. Scholars were to pursue knowledge for its own sake alongside students in whom they had awakened the spirit of scientific investigation. Though they were to pursue knowledge for its own sake, the result would be the development of science, which can never develop fully if pursued only for utilitarian purposes; without a full development of science, a society would lose even some of the utilitarian benefits of that science. Useful knowledge would increase most quickly if scholars were also allowed to pursue useless knowledge.

This was a departure from the development of German higher education in the eighteenth century, which stressed the strict usefulness of knowledge. During the eighteenth century, education had improved, and as Frederick Gregory notes, the improvements "were accomplished in conjunction with the Enlightenment vision of the usefulness of knowledge" (20). However, the usefulness of knowledge for the improvement of society and the state, which was most definitely a theme of the Enlightenment, developed rather narrowly in the German education system, leading to practically oriented institutes and trade schools. To illustrate the spirit of the times, Gregory quotes Wilhelm von Humboldt's predecessor at the Ministry of Education: "From the fullness of my heart I subscribe to the view that instead of universities there should be only gymnasiums and academies for doctors, jurists, etc. To execute this in theory very correct thesis, however, would require so many preparations . . . that for the first fifty years we would still have to endure abnormal universities" (20). This narrowly utilitarian spirit provoked the reaction of the German idealists, who insisted that true education had to be universal in scope and not just concerned with practical trades.

Thus it is possible to argue that Kant, Schelling, Fichte and Schleiermacher were arguing *against* the Enlightenment conception of education, and this is a plausible interpretation depending on what one means by the Enlightenment. For example, Edwina Lawler describes the new "neohumanistic-idealistic concept of the university" developed by the idealists as a reaction against the Enlightenment. "According to rationalistic thinkers of the current order, knowledge had to be both useful and applicable if a rational life in this world was to be realized. The beginning bourgeois society tended to emphasize professional, i.e., practical, education" (3), whereas the "founders of the university in Berlin were against the state as the representative of the utilitarian, practical interests of the Enlightenment" (41). Similarly, Herman Röhrs, in his *The Classical German Concept of the University and Its Influence on Higher Education in the United States*, claims that "the German Enlightenment had led to the teaching of specialized technical knowledge in various professional schools," while "German idealist thinking rebelled against this" (16). This interpretation of the Enlightenment is similar to that of Adorno and Horkheimer and their criticisms of the alleged ultimate Enlightenment value of instrumental rationality.

While this interpretation is fair to some extent, and adequate in describing the way the German Enlightenment proceeded through the governments of the age — "enlightened absolutist" governments — it is hardly representative of the broader Enlightenment described in the first chapter and the implications of broader Enlightenment themes for education. If we consider the Enlightenment not simply as an historical phenomenon but also as a concept, even a project yet to be completed, and one whose values include reason *and* freedom as well as the development of knowledge, then we are led to the conclusion that while the German idealists might have been rebelling against the utilitarian strictures inspired by a narrow interpretation of Enlightenment values by German rulers in the eighteenth century, their rebellion was itself motivated by broader Enlightenment values. My interpretation is analogous in some ways to a reinterpretation of Schleiermacher's work by Earnest Boyer, who argues that "the Enlightenment in general, but especially the German

Enlightenment, has long been viewed too narrowly," and that "there are significant grounds to believe that many of the ideas most associated with Romanticism grew up more as an extension of the *Aufklärung* than as a reaction to it" (203). Though the narrow utilitarian education that developed in eighteenth century Germany was to some extent a positive development, and in line with Enlightenment goals to improve society through useful knowledge, to consider it the fullest development of the Enlightenment in higher education would be an example of a distortion of the Enlightenment similar to those explored by Tzevan Todorov.

We can also consider the study of antiquity and the rise of historical thought in Germany as a decidedly non-utilitarian development of German intellectual culture. The renewed interest in classical culture during the Enlightenment period led Peter Gay to classify the *philosophes* as "modern pagans" (V.1, 8). In her essay on "The Enlightenment and the Rise of Historicism in German Thought," Helen Leibel argues that "the more sophisticated study of Greek and Roman culture which took place in the eighteenth century that resulted in the revolutionary changes in the Western view of history which continue to shape historical and political formulations on both sides of the Atlantic" (359). While the interest in antiquity and the rise of historical thought were not narrowly pragmatic, they were undoubtedly features of the German Enlightenment. Just as Kant and the German idealists were defending the Enlightenment values of reason and freedom as they critiqued problematic Enlightenment thought, so too they were defending the same values as they critiqued the narrowness of contemporary German higher education.

The University of Berlin and the German Model

While the ideal towards which the German idealists aimed was perhaps never completely achieved, and certainly not in the German universities at the time, the arguments of Kant and others led ultimately to the creation of a new university more dedicated to these scholarly ideals than any before it. The University of Berlin, founded in 1810, was the first research university, meaning it was the first university dedicated to the pursuit of knowledge for its own sake in theoretically every domain of study. Its organization provided the model for other German universities and eventually American universities as well.

The founding of the University of Berlin came about as the result of war. Prussia had been at war with Napoleon for years, and in 1806 was decisively defeated at the battles of Jena and Auerstedt. On July 9, 1807, King Friedrich Wilhelm III signed the Treaty of Tilsit, giving up half of his territory to France and Russia. Unfortunately for the intellectual life of Prussia, the lost territory included two of the oldest and best German universities at Jena and Halle. Some professors at the University of Halle requested of Friedrich Wilhelm III that the university be transferred into the current Prussian territory. Supposedly, the King responded, "That is right, that is commendable. What the state has lost in physical strength it must replace with intellectual strength" (quoted in Lawler 2). The same year, Karl Friedrich von Beyme, a minister of the King, asked to continue work planning for a new university in Berlin that had been interrupted by war. Beyme had been heavily influenced by the thinking of Fichte and others on what a proper institution of higher education should do. From 1803 on, Beyme had been soliciting ideas about how a university should be organized from Fichte, Schleiermacher and other prominent thinkers. The King agreed to the founding of the university, and Wilhelm von Humboldt was asked to organize the endeavor (Lawler 1-2, Fallon 5-9), which is why the German model of research university is sometimes called the Humboldtian Model and why Humboldt himself is often considered the "'Father of the University,' where the latter term is meant in the definitive and universal sense" (Fallon 10).

Wilhelm von Humboldt was a fascinating and immensely learned man. He was a liberal intellectual who wrote authoritatively on politics, literature, anthropology, philology, and linguistics, and is perhaps best known in the United States today for his book, *The Limits of State Action*. Humboldt wrote little about the organization and purpose of a university, but it is worth exploring his thoughts about the subject in his 1810 manuscript *"Uber Die Innere Und Äussere Organisation Der Höheren Wissenschaftlichen Anstalten in Berlin"* ("On the internal and external organization of the higher scientific institutions in Berlin"). He considered the purpose of the university as the pursuit of knowledge and learning for its own sake, arguing that "the concept of higher institutions of learning as the summit where everything that happens directly in the interest of the moral culture of the nation comes together, rests on such institutions being designed as places where learning in the deepest and widest sense of the word [*Wissenschaft*] may be cultivated." Universities were also to "treat all knowledge as a not yet wholly solved problem and are therefore never done with investigation and research" (132). These are the most important premises for research universities, because they provide the foundation for everything else, including the necessity of *lehrfrieheit* and *lernfrei-*

heit. The university is very different from the school, which exists to transmit existing knowledge. At universities, knowledge is to be discovered and created, not just transmitted. This also means that a university professor has a very different role than a school teacher. "In the higher institutions, the teacher no longer exists for the sake of the student; both exist for the sake of learning" (133).

The pursuit of knowledge for its own sake must be independent of political control, Humboldt argues, because "inasmuch as all such institutions can attain their purpose only by continual confrontation with the pure idea of learning, the principles ruling their administration are isolation and freedom" (132). In fact, interference by the government to impose a more practical and utilitarian regime on the university are bound to fail. The practical results of pursuing knowledge for its own sake are many, but "the government must always remain conscious that it really neither brings about such results, however desirable, nor can it bring them about. It must remember, in fact, that its intervention is invariably an obstruction to attaining the desired results" (133). In this, Humboldt echoes the thinking of the other German Idealists on the necessity of freedom to pursue pure science to reap the utilitarian benefits that science often brings.

Though the work of the university must be free from political control, and certainly from the strictures of religious authorities, and though it must pursue a pure ideal of learning for its own sake in order to function at all, this does not mean that the university is not serving the state. Humboldt and the other influential thinkers on German higher education had to justify the government supporting something that it could not fully control. However, instead of academic freedom undermining the state, the complete freedom to learn and teach and pursue knowledge for its own sake is *how* the university can best serve the state. To best serve the state, and to produce educated workers for the Prussian state, the government, for its own good, must give up control of the university. Unlike a state bureaucracy, the purpose of a university can never be fulfilled merely through organization. "As soon as one stops searching for knowledge, or if one imagines that it need not be creatively sought in the depths of the human spirit but can be assembled extensively by collecting and classifying facts, everything is irrevocably and forever lost, lost for learning which soon vanishes so far out of the picture that it even leaves language behind like an empty pod, and lost for the state as well" (134). It's the duty of the state to organize universities and let scholars pursue their research, the results of which can sometimes be used for state purposes.

For the most part, Humboldt succeeded in his goal of establishing a university very much like the ideal university imagined by the German idealists. Most importantly, Humboldt managed to establish the university based on three main principles: 1) "unity of research and teaching," 2) "the protection of academic freedom," and 3) "the central importance of the Arts and Sciences (*die philosophische Fakultät*), which revitalized the liberal arts and gave the concept of pure research the significance it is now accorded" (Fallon 28-29). The first principle guaranteed that the university would not be merely a school or a practical institute, but a place where scholarship and scholarly methods would be of central importance. To insure this, Humboldt appointed the best scholars he could find, encouraged their research, and made them "collectively responsible for academic standards and the award of degrees" (28). The protection of academic freedom, which has withstood some blistering attacks in the United States, allowed for the *Lernfreiheit* and *Lehrfreiheit* required to investigate all areas of knowledge. As long as scholars pursue their investigations in accordance with reason and the best scholarly standards, they should be free to follow their investigations wherever they might lead without fear of reprisal from the state or religious authorities, and Humboldt assured that the state would protect the scholars. And finally, the centrality of the philosophy faculty put them in the position Kant had argued they should be in *The Conflict of the Faculties*. It was a sign that their pure research was more important than practical and professional training because it provided the necessary philosophical understanding to undertake professional work more intelligently.

The first research university founded on philosophical ideals turned out to be a success. Pursuing pure research for its own sake greatly expanded the range of human knowledge, and throughout the nineteenth century, the model spread to other German universities. German scholars led the Western world in their erudition and scholarly rigor. This is especially true in historical and literary areas such as history, philology, and Biblical criticism. German universities became renowned as the most academically sophisticated and stimulating institutions of higher education in the West.

By comparison, the colleges and universities in the United States were pale imitations of the higher learning, as Americans who wanted to pursue scholarship past their rather parochial undergraduate educations found. So what did these Americans do? They went to Germany. According to Herman Röhrs, there were "approximately 9000 young people from the United States studying at German universities between 1820 and 1920, notably in Gottingen, Berlin, Halle, Leipzig, and Heidelberg," and while they did not all return to

America and found universities, "the conviction established itself that the German concept of the university, with its central focus on research and the inspiring effect of this bias on instruction, represented a salutary influence in helping the universities in the New World to find their feet" (11). It is to this development that we now turn.

The German Model Comes to America

The transition of American higher education from its provincial and rather narrow origins into the research universities we know today occurred gradually over the course of the nineteenth and well into the twentieth century, but we can point to a handful of illustrative and decisive moments. Gradual reforms at Harvard and the University of Michigan were significant, but the decisive changes come with the founding of Cornell University and especially of the Johns Hopkins University, universities inspired by or founded more or less upon the German model.

In some ways, the first half of the nineteenth century saw a rapid growth in institutions of higher education. In his history of American higher education, Christopher Lucas notes that the number of American colleges rose from nine at the time of the American Revolution to about 250 by the time of the Civil War (17). However, the vast majority of these were decidedly not the type of college or university we commonly consider today. Many of them were founded as sectarian religious colleges, and their efforts at moral formation took precedence over their other educational goals. For example, the "founder of Oberlin College, the Reverend John H. Shepherd, was forthright in announcing that he had come out to the Western Reserve to save the people from 'rum, brandy, gin and whiskey' and to rescue the church from 'Romanists, atheists, Deists, Universalists, and all classes of God's enemies'" (Lucas 120). Obviously, this rhetoric cannot be associated with the Enlightenment, and is exactly the sort of attitude that the *philosophes* had fought in France. That most of these institutions today — Oberlin or Kenyon or numerous others — have vastly different goals more in line with the pursuit of truth than the inculcation of religious doctrine, speaks to the influence of Enlightenment thinking via the German model of higher education.

The tenor of some of these institutions was overwhelmingly religious, specifically Protestant and Christian, signified by the activities of the students and the rules of the colleges. Today, we think of Harvard as one of the leading secular research universities in the world, with students who strenuously challenge themselves and their culture, whereas in the nineteenth century Harvard students "devoted much of their free time debating such weighty questions as whether any sin was absolutely unpardonable or whether sexual intercourse after a formal marital engagement qualified as fornication." Similarly, in the first half of the nineteenth century at Yale, the rule was that "'if any student shall profess or endeavor to propagate a disbelief in the divine authority of the Holy Scriptures, and shall persist therein after admonition, he shall no longer be a member of the College'" (Lucas 129). The freedom to learn and to teach necessary for a university in the German sense was severely restricted.

Many of these colleges emphasized a classical liberal arts curriculum, though that was not true of all of them. For example, according to John Thelin's *History of American Higher Education*, a study of the student diaries and memoirs of South Carolina College — the predecessor to the University of South Carolina — shows that the "formal curriculum emphasized a didactic method centered on the specific philosophy of states' rights and nullification theory" (48). Some others offered instruction in the sciences, and gradually modern languages were introduced at selected schools. Military academies such as West Point or the Citadel provided significant engineering schools (59). While some universities had schools of law or medicine or perhaps even the odd graduate program, none had complete graduate schools in the liberal arts and sciences resembling those in the German universities.

The American students at German universities were aware of how different German universities were. For example, James Morgan Hart — who studied at Leipzig, Marburg, and Berlin in the 1860s and later taught at Cornell — explained to Americans what the Germans meant by a university. "To the German mind the collective idea of a university implies a *Zweck*, an object of study, and two *Bedingungen*, or conditions. The object is *Wissenschaft*; the conditions are *Lehrfreiheit* and *Lernfreiheit*. By *Wissenschaft* the Germans mean knowledge in the most exalted sense of that term, namely, the ardent, methodical, independent search after truth in any and all of its forms, but wholly irrespective of utilitarian application" (Hofstadter 571). There were no American institutions that could compare at all favorably to the best German universities because none were based on the ideals of *Lehrfreiheit* and *Lernfreiheit* in the service of *Wissenschaft*, or the freedom to teach and learn in the service of knowledge for its own sake.

In the generation after the Civil War, things began to change. Christopher Lucas lists the reformers: "men such as Andrew D. White of Cornell, John Howard Raymond of Vassar, William Watts Folwell and Cyrus Northrup at Minnesota, William B. Rogers of the Massachusetts Institute of Technology, Walter B. Hill at Georgia, James H. Kirkland at Vanderbilt, William Pepper at Pennsylvania, Daniel Coit Gilman of Hopkins, and Charles W. Eliot at Harvard." Lucas characterizes these men as impatient and aggressive, with a shared goal of "refashioning American higher education in a new mold: that of the university" (143). Within a couple of generations, numerous American institutions of higher education had been so refashioned.

It is worth examining the thoughts of some of the early champions of the university in America. For example, Henry P. Tappan, president of the University of Michigan, was a strong proponent of German-style universities and wanted to remake Michigan along their lines. According to Herman Röhrs, Tappan thus created the "first graduate program in the United States" and appointed as a professor of history Andrew White, whose "contribution to the development of Ann Arbor was a decisive one" (77). Andrew White, in his turn, was the founding president of Cornell University, while his college friend Daniel Coit Gilman was the founding president of Johns Hopkins.

Tappan's thinking on the nature and purpose of a university should sound familiar. In an 1858 speech, Tappan opined that:

> Of all mere human institutions there are none so important and mighty in their influence as Universities; because, when rightly constituted, they are made up of the most enlightened, and the choicest spirits of our race; they embrace the means of all human culture, and they act directly upon the fresh and upspringing manhood of a nation. To them must be traced science, literature, and art; the furniture of religious faith; the

lights of industry; the moving forces of civilization; and the brotherly unity of humanity.

It would be difficult to find rhetoric that grandiose even from Fichte. Universities consist of books and scholars, and where "you collect the treasures of knowledge [books], and the men who know how to use and apply them, there, and there only, you have properly a university." Tappan reiterated the Germans' insistence that the enterprise worked only if it were independent from political or religious influence, from any "barbarous attempt to harness the winged Pegasus to the drag of beggarly elements." Universities could only do their work if the scholars were left alone to do their work, since freedom was "the grand characteristic of University Education" (Hofstadter 517).

The next milestone in the slow progress of the German model through American higher education was the founding of Cornell University by Ezra Cornell and Andrew D. White in 1865. Ezra Cornell had founded Western Union and made a fortune, eventually retiring to focus on philanthropic efforts and stating as one goal (and now Cornell's motto): "I would found an institution where any person can find instruction in any study." White was the founding president, and he had been particularly influenced by the thought and work of Henry B. Tappan while he, White, was a professor at Michigan. White noted in his autobiography that Tappan was "greatly impressed by the large and liberal system of the German universities," and wanted to develop something similar in the United States (Hofstadter 546). This at a time when the leading colleges of the east were as "stagnant as a Spanish convent." The University of Michigan under Tappan was nonsectarian and had a variety of courses of instruction as well as a choice of study. White also complains that Tappan was often unsuccessful in gaining funding for the reforms he sought to make because of the sectarian demagogues in the Michigan legislature, who were unimpressed by Prussian universities and much beholden to the state's sectarian colleges.

White wanted to found a university based on the German principles. As he studied in Europe, he dreamed of creating a new university. His dream university would be "beautiful and dignified," like Oxford or Cambridge, but with a much broader range of study. He was also particular that his university would be free of the control of any religious organization, and with no religious tests for its professors (550). Eventually, he found a benefactor in Ezra Cornell and in the United States government, which in 1862 had passed the first Morrill Act. The Morrill Act granted federal land to the states, with the proceeds from its sale going to the "maintenance of at least one college where the leading object shall be, without excluding other scientific and classical studies and including military tactics, to teach such branches of learning as are related to agriculture and the mechanic arts, in such manner as the legislatures of the States may respectively prescribe, in order to promote the liberal and practical education of the industrial classes in the several pursuits and professions in life" (7 U.S.C. § 304). Cornell donated $500,000 of his own money for the founding of the university, with the rest coming from the federal land grant money, which White had secured for Cornell despite the many sectarian colleges in New York fighting for the money and the accusations that Ezra Cornell was founding an "aristocratic" university "for the propagation of 'atheism' and 'infidelity'" (Hofstadter 556, 558). As always, proponents of enlightenment had to battle the forces of irrationality and willful ignorance.

The sectarian and narrow-minded resistance to education that might be at odds with religious ideals, though not with evidence or human reason, is sometimes frightening and sometimes comical. White recounted the case of a young clergyman who visited his private library wanting to "borrow some works showing the more recent tendencies of liberal thought." White showed him his books, where, "by the side of the works of Bossuet and Fenelon and Thomas Arnold and Robertson of Brighton, he found those of Channing, Parker, Renan, Strauss, and the men who, in the middle years of the last century, were held to represent advanced thought." The man left in a hurry without borrowing any books, and White next heard from him when the clergyman published in his denominational newspaper an "eloquent denunciation" of White for even *owning* such books (559). Condemning books without reading them or avoiding them because one disagrees with them is a sure sign that one has escaped the influence of the Enlightenment. Despite the attacks on Cornell for not being narrow or sectarian in its educational goals, White managed to found a university supporting the study of theoretical and utilitarian subjects broadly in line with the Enlightenment and the German model.

Reform at Harvard provided another milestone. Charles W. Eliot, one of the major reformers of American higher education in the nineteenth century, led the development of Harvard University from a relatively traditional college with a few graduate programs to a modern research university during his forty years as the university president. From his inaugural address in 1869, it is obvious that Eliot was heavily influenced by the German model of higher education.

> The endless controversies whether language, philosophy, mathematics, or science supplies the best mental training, whether general education should be chiefly literary or chiefly scientific, have no practical regard for us to-day. This University recognizes no real antagonism between literature and science, and consents to no such narrow alternatives as mathematics or classics, science or metaphysics. We would have them all, and at their best. (Hofstadter 602)

All subjects are worthy of study, and all *should* be studied somewhere at a university. This is in stark contrast to the popular notion — then and now — that higher education should focus merely on the practical, the utilitarian, and the vocational. Eliot did not dismiss such education, but in his address argued that practical application of knowledge was not a concern at a university until the level of professional education. "Poetry and philosophy and science," he said, "do indeed conspire to promote the material welfare of mankind; but science no more than poetry finds its best warrant in its utility," because "truth and right are above utility in all realms of thought and action" (602). He did not see the need to add the justification of Fichte and Humboldt, that only by studying pure science could practical applications result.

The battle between a traditional liberal arts education and more utilitarian training has raged in the United States for almost two centuries now. An early salvo in defense of a liberal education comes from the *Reports on the Course of Instruction in Yale College by a Committee of the Corporation and the Aca-*

demical Faculty, usually referred to as the 1828 "Yale Report." The "Yale Report" defended a classical curriculum, arguing that there are two important parts of education, disciplining the mind and stocking it with knowledge. Since disciplining the mind is more important and fundamental, a college education should "call into daily and vigorous exercise the faculties of the student." The curriculum should focus on what is

> best calculated to teach the art of fixing the attention, directing the train of thought, analyzing a subject proposed for investigation; following, with accurate discrimination, the course of argument; balancing nicely the evidence presented to the judgment; awakening, elevating, and controlling the imagination; arranging, with skill, the treasures which memory gathers; rousing and guiding the powers of genius. (Reports 7)

Such habits had to be formed over time and with intensive study, and while they may have utilitarian benefits, such study is not utilitarian in itself.

Colleges that did not offer utilitarian training were often criticized. For example, a newspaper editorial in Georgia argued that "We are now living in a different age, an age of practical utility, one in which the State University does not, and cannot supply the demands of the state. The times require practical men, civil engineers, to take charge of public roads, railroads, mines, scientific agriculture" (quoted in Lucas 135). Eventually, many universities offered a range of general education and professional training, but the debate is apparently neverending. Anytime you read a news article about whether attending college is worth the cost, or see any purely economic analysis of the cost of higher education based upon the earning power of college graduates versus non-college graduates, you are seeing the education / vocational training debate that has persisted for two hundred years.

In his inaugural address, Eliot was definitely arguing against the narrowness of purely utilitarian training in favor of the German model of the pursuit of knowledge for its own sake. And yet we should note that he *also* argued against the ultimate conclusions of the "Yale Report." While the "Yale Report" argued vigorously against considering utilitarian and practical subjects as part of a liberal education, it was also arguing against any changes in what might be considered liberal education, including changes that might result from adopting reforms based upon the German model, and specifically doubted whether "they are models to be copied in every feature, by our American colleges" (21).

One feature of German education that the "Yale Report" definitely thought should not be copied was *lehrfreiheit*, the freedom of the students to study what they like. While admitting, correctly, that college students in the United States were typically younger than their German counterparts, and that American colleges were more equivalent to German *gymnasia* rather than universities, the "Yale Report" used this to reject any broad freedom of study. Students could pursue their own studies only after much plodding through the common classical curriculum. While there would be a core curriculum constituting a liberal education, modern languages would not be part of it. The acquisition of a modern language was considered an "accomplishment, rather than as a necessary acquisition," and to study them before studying ancient languages was to "reverse the order of nature" (39), as if it were somehow natural that native speakers of the non-classical language English should study Greek rather than German.

Instead of a "variety of classes," the curriculum should confine itself to the "single object of a well proportioned and thorough course of study," that is, the study of classical languages. Such study is the best course for a liberal education because "every faculty of the mind is employed, . . . not only the memory, judgment, and reasoning powers, but the taste and fancy are occupied and improved" (36). Not only is a classical curriculum the best path to liberal education, but the only path, and the report goes on to claim that if the college conferred "degrees upon students for their attainments in modern literature only, it would be to declare *that* to be a liberal education, which the world will not acknowledge to deserve the name" (41). (English majors, take note!) If such a radical innovation were to occur, the faculty believed they would be "considered visionaries in education, ignorant of its true design and objects, and unfit for their places" (42). The "Yale Report" opposed treating college education as professional education or job training, but it also opposed any freeing of the liberal arts curriculum from the traditional focus on classical studies.

At Harvard forty years later, Eliot was battling against the idea that higher education should concern itself only with the utilitarian, but also against the traditional notion of a fixed classical curriculum, and the latter battle was probably more controversial among educators than the former. In his "Inaugural Address," he attacked the idea of a "uniform curriculum" that forced everyone to study "the same subjects in the same proportions" without regards to their abilities or preferences. He notes the system was still prevalent in American colleges, and had "vigorous defenders" because it had the "merit of simplicity." "So had the school methods of our grandfathers — one primer, one catechism, one rod for all children" (608). Eliot considered this to be folly, and argued that students should be allowed to pursue the intellectual interests best suited to them. Society needs a division of labor in intellectual work as in any other, since the "civilization of a people may be inferred from the variety of its tools." The more developed tools are, the more they are adapted to specific purposes. In the same way, a more specialized society requires more specialized education. For that reason, Eliot vowed "to establish, improve, and extend the elective systems" (610). With the adoption of the elective system at Harvard, a crucial principle of the German university model — freedom to learn — gained another important foothold in American higher education.

The founding of Johns Hopkins in 1876 was another significant step, since it "was planned as a university rather than a college," and its German-style graduate school provided a clear Americanized model later followed by other institutions, whether they were founding similar schools as with the University of Chicago, or layering a graduate school on top of a more English style college as at Yale (French 1). Johns Hopkins was a wealthy wholesale merchant and venture capitalist in Baltimore, and in his will he left $7,000,000 to found a university and a hospital. As John C. French notes in his history of the Johns Hopkins University, Hopkins left the money to found a university, but left no guidance about what sort of university it was supposed to be. The part of the will mentioning the university is concerned primarily with the handling of the endowment, specifically restricting the university corporation from selling the stock or using the capital left to fund the university. University funding was to come from interest, dividends, and student fees (French 463), but what sort of university should be funded remained open.

The man most responsible for founding the Johns Hopkins University along German lines was Daniel Coit Gilman, at that time the president of the University of California at Berkeley. Just as another wealthy philanthropist had given his college friend Andrew White the means to fund a new university, Hopkins' legacy allowed Gilman to do the same. The founding principles of the Johns Hopkins University as Gilman expounded them are worth quoting at length. The university, he believed,

> should forever be free from the influences of ecclesiasticism or partisanship, as those terms are used in narrow and controversial senses; that all departments of learning — mathematical, scientific, literary, historical, philosophical — should be promoted, as far as the funds at command will permit, the new departments of research receiving full attention, while the traditional are not slighted; that the instructions should be as thorough, as advanced and as special as the intellectual condition of the country will permit; that the glory of the University should rest upon the character of the teachers and scholars here brought together, and not upon their number, nor upon the buildings constructed for their use. (Hofstadter 755)

This encapsulates the ideal principles of the Humboldtian university quite well. Every possible subject is worthy of investigation, not just traditional subjects or those approved by religious or political authorities, and the investigations should be as advanced as possible. In another place, Gilman explains that the "professors should have ample time to carry on the higher work for which they had shown themselves qualified," since in a research university the first principle is to advance scholarship, not simply to pass knowledge on to undergraduates. However, this would also show even undergraduates what research really involves, and by studying with the practicing scholars, students "were shown how to discover the limits of the known; how to extend, even by minute accretions, the realm of knowledge; how to cooperate with other men in the prosecution of inquiry; and how to record in exact language, and on the printed page, the results attained" (646).

Intellectual freedom, a central value for librarians — and for similar reasons — was also central to the founding of the Johns Hopkins University. Gilman was emphatic that Hopkins was devoted to the "discovery and promulgation of the truth," and that it could not be a true university if it allowed its scholars to be limited by sectarian or political restrictions. "As the spirit of the University should be that of intellectual freedom in the pursuit of truth." Gilman wrote, "and of the broadest charity toward those from whom we differ in opinion it is certain that sectarian and partisan preferences should have no control in the selection of teachers, and should not be apparent in their official work" (845). Thus Hopkins, along with Cornell, was a new thing in American higher education — a university devoted to the pursuit of knowledge for its own sake wherever that knowledge might lead, rather than a college founded to train ministers or an academy to promote practical knowledge. Truth was defined by reason, not revelation. Furthermore, with the founding of various scholarly journals, the scholars were not only free to pursue their investigations, but encouraged to publish their results to share with other scholars (647). The German research university had arrived in America.

The German model was also Americanized in a way that allowed for an increased development of research. In their book on *The Rise of American Research Universities*, Hugh Graham and Nancy Diamond argue that the German model developed a distinctly American cast for various reasons, including organizing graduate schools on top of undergraduate colleges, decentralization, pluralism, the existence of private universities, and a national academic market, none of which were the case with German universities (11). They also explain that the German research universities were "based on continental Europe's 'chair' system," with a prominent professor directing a research institute. They conclude that, "on the whole, the system proved too rigid to accommodate the accelerating pace of scientific change. While American research universities did not organize themselves exactly like German universities in every detail, nevertheless they were motivated by the same ideal of pursuing knowledge for its own sake.

The Rise of the American Research Library

1876, the year the Johns Hopkins University was founded, coincided with the centennial of the founding of the United States of America in a Declaration of Independence much inspired by Enlightenment thought. It was a significant year for libraries as well. In his history of the American university library, Arthur Hamlin lists the significant library-related events of that year. The American Library Association (ALA) was founded, as well as the *Library Journal*, still a significant publication in librarianship. The Library Bureau of the United States government came into being, and the Bureau of Education published the extensive survey, *Public Libraries in the United States of America: their History, Condition, and Management*. In addition to his influence in the founding of ALA, Melvil Dewey — at the time the chief librarian at Columbia University — also published the outline of his Dewey Decimal System. The same year saw the "publication of Cutter's *Rules for a Printed Dictionary and Catalogue*, which did for librarians roughly what *Systema Naturae* of Linnaeus had done for botanists a hundred and fifty years earlier, and unlike Linnaeus, had immediate acceptance" (45-46). If we consider this in the light of Henry Steele Commager's enthusiastic listing of classification schemes, including Linnaeus', we can consider 1876 as the year that Enlightenment scientific principles were finally applied to the organization of information. The rise of the research university and the spread of the research ideal throughout higher education meant that the organization of librarians and their organization of books and information came at just the right time.

Throughout this chapter, you might have been wondering why there was little mention of libraries, which might seem odd since this is a book about libraries. Academic libraries are dependent on their parent institutions for their form and motivation. Throughout the history of American higher education prior to the introduction and spread of the research university, college libraries were just not that important. Often they were open but a few hours a week, and never at night because of the serious concern that candles and paper together created a fire hazard in the wooden buildings. The librarians were usually poorly paid scholars or former students. Most of the libraries had very small collections of books, which were either lent sparingly to students or not at all. Since instruction was dependent on studying a few classical texts closely, or through recitation from textbooks, there was hardly any need for academic libraries to support the curricula of the colleges. The books that students really wanted were rarely in the library or the curriculum anyway, hence the rise of student literary societies that built libraries of their own, which in the twentieth century were often merged with university libraries.

As colleges transitioned into research universities dedicated to the pursuit of knowledge in multiple fields, then and only then did they require the large academic libraries that became common in the twentieth century. And as the research ideal spread to the extent that even professors at small colleges were often expected to produce at least some original research for tenure and promotion, so the national network of American university and college libraries sharing information among themselves developed. In the past, scholarship had been an individual endeavor, but with the rise of the German model, as Hamlin puts it, "the new university provided a center of concentration, the association of other scholars, research materials, laboratories, and means of publishing. Scholarship, rather than teaching, became the vital core of the new profession" (47), and the foundation or development of research universities like Michigan, Harvard, Cornell, and Hopkins created the need for large research libraries to serve research-oriented goals. This change was not always fully supported, since serious research libraries are always expensive to build and maintain relative to the financial standards of the time. Nevertheless, eventually, with the spread of the research ideal "generally came rapidly increasing annual budgets for books and journals, for employment of library staffs headed by professional librarians, and for the erection of costly buildings designed not only to hold large collections but to provide good working conditions for students, scholars, and librarians" (48).

The generation or two after the founding of the Johns Hopkins University and the creation of the first national professional organization of libraries saw the emerging development of the academic library from small beginnings to the institutions we have today, where even small colleges might have collections of 300,000 or more books, and large research libraries many millions of books. To a great extent, the biggest change was that libraries started actively buying books. This might seem a trivial point, because of course libraries buy books. However, before the rise of the research university, and its concomitant research library, there was really little need for academic libraries to buy books, or to have what librarians call a collection development policy. Collection development, the librarian's term of art for buying stuff for the library, became a priority, and even a necessity, only as scholars needed books and journals for their research. Only then did libraries begin trying to buy books in given areas of scholarship, often trying to buy everything in areas relevant to current research. As the research agenda spread, librarians had to figure out just what was needed and organize ways to acquire the necessary material. Today, much of that work is done by large book vendors, who develop elaborate profiles with academic libraries and then set up "approval plans" to automatically ship every book that meets the library's criteria to the library. In the beginning of research libraries, the purchasing apparatus was much less robust.

Arthur Hamlin summarizes the dramatic changes in libraries during this period, including a shift from conserving and protecting books to facilitating their use by scholars, the development of personal service in using the library, the recognition of the library's educational role on campus, the rise of classifying books by subject, the necessity of bibliographic description of the books to make them findable, the creation of departmental libraries, and increasing cooperation with other libraries, especially through interlibrary loan (48-49). Today it is almost inconceivable that academic libraries were tiny affairs where books were often organized on the shelves in the order they arrived ("accession order" in library jargon) or where there might be no library catalog at all, but perhaps only the barest listing of the contents of the library. It is also difficult to imagine an academic library with no librarians to help library users.

The major changes leading to the current shape of academic libraries came in two parts — services and collections — both of which were woefully inadequate by today's standards. The services came first. For example, Harvard had the first public card catalog in the country, created during the 1860s by Ezra Abbot and Charles Ammi Cutter, but even then books were tedious for library users to retrieve. Harvard librarian Justin Winsor, to whom Hamlin attributes "the creed that a library justified its existence by use" and "that the purpose of a book was to be read," instituted a new paging system that made it easier for students to get books. Though now many academic libraries have open stacks, meaning that students can go to the library shelves to get books themselves, many large research libraries still have closed stacks, including the main library at Harvard (50). However, most academic libraries found ways to make their books more accessible to scholars.

Melvil Dewey continued his crusade to modernize librarianship as the head of the Columbia College Library after 1883. He extended the weekly open hours of the library from ten to eighty-four, allowed students to retrieve their own books, and created a modern card catalog. By having lectures given on how to use the library, he also started an early library instruction program. Perhaps most importantly for library service, he created the first library reference department. Much of this was overseen, in Hamlin's words, by "six attractive, intelligent, library assistants, all recent graduates of Wellesley, now known to fame as 'the Wellesley half dozen'" (51). According to Dewey's biographer Wayne Wiegand, "hiring college-educated women fit Dewey's concept of librarianship's professional boundaries." Educated women would have a suitable character and be able to determine the best reading for the library. As Weigand also notes, "because they were grateful for new professional opportunities, they would also come for less money," so while the man hired to oversee the politics and history collections was paid $1,000 a year, the Wellesley Half Dozen were paid but $500 (85). This can be interpreted in a number of ways. Hiring women for professional jobs was a relatively enlightened step, since it was early for women to take on professional roles in America, but it also started a trend of paying women less than men for similar library work that is only recently nearing its end. The average salary for female librarians in research libraries in 2010 was 96.2% of the average salary of male librarians, up from 87% in 1981, and obviously up significantly from the 1880s (Kyrillidou 11). One could argue that equal pay for equal work based on the equal rights of women and men is another Enlightenment-inspired principle slowly being achieved.

Over time, one of the most important services to develop, and one without which this book could certainly not have been written, was interlibrary loan. The first issue of the *Library Journal* in 1876 published a letter to the editor by Samuel Swett Green, the librarian of the Free Public Library in Worcester, Massachusetts. Green argued that libraries lending "books to each other for short periods of time" would bring great benefit to libraries and their users (Schlup 23). Hamlin, writing in 1981, points out that new idea grew "gradually into the practice of interlibrary loan which now involves literally millions of transactions annually by academic and public libraries" (53). According to a study by the U.S. Department of Education, in 2008 11,095,168 total documents were loaned by academic libraries in the United States (Table 1). Academic libraries, and to some extent public libraries, have developed possibly the most robust library lending network in the world, where just about any published document can be obtained on a temporary loan by just about any scholar at any college or university in America. This network might be under threat as ebooks and other documents with extensive digital rights management (DRM) continue to grow as a portion of library collections, but there can be no doubt that interlibrary loan has been a remarkable success in library cooperation.

Libraries also began cooperating in building their collections during this era. It has always been the case that no library, even the richest, can afford to buy everything a complete research library needs to collect, since research libraries in total tend to collect a significant amount of the published and much unpublished material from every region on earth. Cooperative lending through interlibrary loan and cooperative collection development have allowed the dollars of every research library to stretch further. The first cooperative collection arrangements were between urban libraries, such as Harvard with the Boston Public Library (Hamlin 54). New York City provides another example, and by 1911 the Columbia University Library "had established what amounted to a cooperative collection development program with the New

York Public Library, by which the New York Public Library submitted its newest acquisitions for Columbia faculty to review for purchase by the University" (Columbia). Such arrangements eventually spread regionally and even nationally. Cooperative collection development has been less successful than cooperative lending for a variety of reasons, often enough because of budget constraints, but several efforts have succeeded in collecting rare material that any single library would not have collected. For example, the Farmington Plan, administered by the Association of Research Libraries (founded in 1932), was a cooperative effort to acquire books from a variety of European countries after World War II had disrupted the European book trade, and thus the research needs of scholars studying Europe. It "was a voluntary agreement under which some 60 libraries attempted to bring to the United States at least one copy of each new foreign monograph of research value," although eventually a variety of tensions led to its discontinuation in 1972 (Drake 208). Several research libraries in the Midwest formed what was to become the Center for Research Libraries (CRL); its purpose was

> to establish and maintain an educational, literary, scientific, charitable and research interlibrary center; to provide and promote cooperative, auxiliary services for one or more non-profit educational, charitable and scientific institutions; to establish, conduct and maintain a place or places for the deposit, storage, care, delivery and exchange of books ... and other articles containing written, printed, or recorded matter. (quoted in Center)

Today the Center for Research Libraries acquires materials from all over the world, preserves them, and makes them accessible to scholars through interlibrary loan.

As scholars required more and more material and produced more themselves, collections at most academic libraries expanded at a remarkable pace that quickly outgrew the capacity of libraries to hold them. The Princeton University Library provides a typical case study. When James McCosh became president of Princeton University in 1868, he was shocked by the condition of the library, saying that "'it should be a place of activity for both professors and students. . . . How could there be a truly intellectual life among the undergraduates if their reading was confined to textbooks.'" He hired a new librarian, Frederick Vinton, to build the collection, and over a "fifteen-year period the fourteen-thousand-volume collection of 1868 had quadrupled to sixty thousand" (Hamlin 52). By 1920 that figure was to reach almost half a million items. At that rapid pace, it is hardly surprising how quickly libraries were built or expanded. Princeton built a new library — the Chancellor Green Library — in 1875, an octagonal building with shelves and study carrels surrounding an open area, "considered by many to be a model of future library space." Within twenty years that library was full, and the Pyne Library was added to it. By the mid-1940s, the 1.2 million volume collection exceeded the capacity of both buildings, and the Harvey S. Firestone Memorial Library opened in 1948. (Princeton was a bit behind some other universities, many of which built large central libraries during the 1920s and 1930s.) The Firestone Library was expanded in 1971, and *again* in 1988 (Princeton). Firestone Library has been at capacity since 2000, and further expansion is avoidable only because of an offsite, high-density storage system shared with the Columbia University Library and the New York Public Library that can currently hold up to ten million volumes in five modules (ReCap). Such a story is typical at most large university libraries, and a recurring theme in Wayne Weigand's *Leaders in American Academic Librarianship: 1925-1975* is how much time those leaders spent overseeing library construction projects.

Currently academic libraries face a number of threats and problems, but those problems stray too far from our topic. Academic libraries, from large research libraries to smaller college libraries, are products of the Enlightenment and its promotion of reason and freedom. The pursuit of knowledge for its own sake wherever it might lead, the examination of every possible topic in the light of reason, and the freedom to publish that research to the world — the underlying principles of modern universities — led to the inevitable creation of the libraries capable of supporting those goals. While scholars investigated, examined, experimented and wrote and wrote and wrote, academic librarians worked to acquire, preserve, organize, and make accessible the materials they needed, and in the process built up a national network of cooperative collections and services in the support of scholarship. Though I focused on the development of research universities and their libraries, this network supports researchers at all institutions of higher education, and is just about as close to a universal library in practice as we have seen since the Library at Alexandria.

CHAPTER III

Public Libraries *and the* Political Enlightenment

JUST AS ACADEMIC LIBRARIES of whatever size are shaped by and dependent upon the colleges or universities they serve, public libraries are shaped by and dependent upon the communities they serve. Unlike academic libraries, however, public libraries are created as institutions in themselves, rather than as supportive adjuncts to some larger institution, unless that larger institution is a municipality or even a democratic state. The relationship between public libraries and Enlightenment thought is both obvious and obscure. The original motivations of public libraries are clearly inspired by Enlightenment ideas, but the history of public libraries, which I will explore in brief, shows a much more complicated relationship to the Enlightenment. However, despite later twentieth century controversies about the purpose of public libraries, in the

United States they were almost always founded as a means of spreading education and enlightenment necessary to the citizens of a democratic republic.

The Enlightenment gave us a belief in the value of using the scientific investigation of nature and society in order to improve the lot of humanity, as well as a belief in the value of individual human freedom within a republican political system. The philosophical Enlightenment, as I have interpreted it here, provided the rationale for the creation and development of academic libraries, primarily large research libraries, but also for the well integrated system of academic libraries that serves students and scholars at institutions of higher education great and small throughout the country. With the rise of research universities came enormous developments in knowledge creation, and this knowledge was stored mostly in academic libraries.

Research universities were but the eventual fruit of the Enlightenment desire for knowledge, and the Enlightenment-inspired desire to investigate nature and society and create new knowledge had already inspired a revolution in thought by the early eighteenth century. The desire for self-education, and later the belief in the necessity for self-education among citizens of a democratic republic, led to the creation of public, or at least social libraries, both from below and from above. For a thorough history of the origins of public libraries in the United States, there are numerous texts to consult, including classics such as Jesse Shera's *Foundations of the Public Library* and Sidney Ditzion's *Arsenals of a Democratic Culture*. A complete history would take too much space here, so instead I will focus on especially relevant episodes in the development of public libraries.

The Library Company of Philadelphia

It should come as no surprise that one of the earliest American libraries serving a function similar to that of a public library was the brainchild of one of the key American thinkers of the Enlightenment, Benjamin Franklin. If we think of a public library as a library that anyone can use, then the Library Company of Philadelphia, founded by Franklin and others in 1731, was not a public library as such. In that sense, public libraries would not exist until the nineteenth century. The Library Company is generally considered a "social" rather than a public library, but its genesis and the inspiration it provided give it a necessary place in our story.

Franklin had for some time gathered with other young artisans in Philadelphia in a debating society they called the Junto. The qualifying test for a potential member of the Junto is worth quoting to show the nature of the group.

> Any person to be qualified — to stand up, and lay his hand upon his breast, and be asked these questions, viz.:
>
> 1st Have you any particular disrespect to any present member? Answer: I have not.
> 2d Do you sincerely declare that you love mankind in general, of what profession or religion soever? Ans. I do.
> 3d Do you think any person ought to be harmed in his body, name, or goods, for mere speculative opinions, or his external way of worship? Ans. No.
> 4th Do you love truth for truth's sake, and will you endeavor impartially to find and receive it yourself, and communicate it to others? Ans. Yes. (Franklin 171)

In these questions and the desired answers we can see the influence of the Enlightenment on the Junto: a love of humanity in general, an aversion to sectarianism and religious bigotry, and a love of truth for truth's sake. In his *Autobiography*, Franklin discusses the rules for the group guiding their weekly meetings. His rules required that members in rotation "should produce one or more queries on any point of Morals, Politics, or Natural Philosophy, to be discuss'd by the company," and every three months read one of their own essays to the group on any subject. The debates were "to be conducted in the sincere spirit of inquiry after truth, without fondness for dispute, or desire of victory; and, to prevent warmth, all expressions of positiveness in opinions, or direct contradiction, were after some time made contraband, and prohibited under small pecuniary penalties" (168). The Junto would be an uncomfortable group for anyone holding stubbornly to religious or political prejudices that could not withstand the light of calm and reasoned debate.

Naturally enough, such a debating society needed to consult books to confirm or dispute assertions. In the early eighteenth century, there was no publicly available library in Philadelphia, and books themselves were expensive and hard to come by, especially for young and relatively impecunious artisans. In 1729, Franklin had suggested that each of the Junto members contribute books to a common library they could all consult, but the initial resulting library was a failure because of its small size and the hard use some books underwent, and within a year the library discontinued. Franklin then began a project, his first "of a public nature," that he was still proud of decades later as he wrote his autobiography. He drew up a plan for a subscription library that would be larger in scope than the dozen members of the Junto. The initial subscription was "forty shillings each to begin with, and ten shillings a year for fifty years, the term our company was to continue." His predicted time frame was too short, since the Library Company still exists today. Eventually the Library Company received a charter from the proprietors of Pennsylvania (then obviously still a colony), and a grant of land to build a library upon. In Franklin's words, the Library Company "was the mother of all the North American subscription libraries, now so numerous. It is become a great thing itself, and continually increasing."

Though the Library Company itself was not the sole inspiration for such libraries in America, the idea spread throughout the colonies. Jesse Shera gives the figures for New England, where the total number of such libraries expanded from four in 1731 to fifty-one by 1780 (55). In his autobiography, Franklin claims that "these libraries have improved the general conversation of the Americans, made the common tradesmen and farmers as intelligent as most gentlemen from other countries, and perhaps have contributed in some degree to the stand so generally made throughout the colonies in defence of their privileges" (194). For Franklin, at least, the spread of knowledge through libraries led to both personal and political enlightenment.

A major goal of Franklin and the Library Company was to help people improve themselves in practical ways, not just spiritual, and this motivation played itself out in the selection of books for the Library. Whereas early libraries in America, such as they were, often enough consisted of religious and theological tracts, the Library Company's collection had relatively few books on religion. As with the Junto, the Library Company was non-sectarian in its accumulation of knowledge. Franklin biographer Joseph Lemay analyzes and lists the specific books that the Library Company gradually acquired, but a subject classification of the first batch of books purchased gives us an idea of the scope of the collection. According to LeMay, Franklin classified the books "into the following categories: History, Architecture, Mathematics, Morality, Geography, Physick, Anatomy, Natural Philosophy, Botany, Politicks, "The Compleat Tradesman" (no category), Animals, Chronology, Logics, Philology, "Wood's Institutes" (no category), and catalogues." Religion did not even figure as a subject, though several sciences did. The largest categories were History with nine titles, then Morality, but even the titles under Morality were typical of the Enlightenment rather than a religious library collection: "Spectators, Guardians, Tatlers, Puffendorf's Law of Nature &c, Addison's Works in 12mo, Memorable Things of Socrates, and the Turkish Spy" (101). The urbane and secular morality of the Spectator has nothing in common with the dogmatic morality of a religious sect. Almost all the books were in English as well, because the library was for practical working people wanting to improve themselves, and not just scholars.

Franklin had noted that this was his first public project. The Junto fit perfectly into the Enlightenment emphasis on self-education, an American instance of what the Germans during the Enlightenment called *Bildung*, which signified "a continuous process of passive formation and active forming of individuals who would instinctively act in the common interest to preserve the civil liberties necessary for the cultivation of the moral arts" (Cocalis 41). According to Joseph LeMay, Franklin "founded the Library Company," like the Junto, "partly as a means of self-education and partly as a means to spread education among his friends," but "unlike the Junto, it was meant to be a useful means of self-education for others in the future," and "a manifestation of Franklin's belief in democracy and egalitarianism" (123). Literary historian Larzer Ziff had emphasized the social advantages of books during the eighteenth century, but LeMay argues that the social advantages were merely a by-product, and that the "availability of books and the possibility of self-education meant that the common man did not automatically have to be satisfied in the roles he found himself by birth and early training." The Library Company established a relationship between education and egalitarianism, and according to LeMay, "Franklin hoped that education could transform the hierarchical world in which he had been born into one where persons could create themselves" (122).

Education and the Republic

The relationship between education and equality was a natural feature of a country that was founded on Enlightenment principles, the first nation founded as an idea. Though America has never been completely egalitarian in fact, this egalitarian rhetoric and the movements it continues to inspire show the resilience of the idea among many Americans. Though not always so egalitarian in inspiration, the belief in the ability of individuals to improve themselves through self-education persists throughout the history of public libraries. While Franklin's Library Company was not available to all the citizens of Philadelphia, the ideas behind it continued to form part of the inspiration for public libraries even into the twentieth century. The motto of the Library Company was "*Communiter bona profundere deum est*," "To pour forth benefits for the common good is divine." Such could be the motto of any public library.

Self-education served a larger purpose than the very practical one of allowing those without the means of education to improve themselves personally and professionally. It was also considered a necessity in a democratic republic, and once the colonists "stood in defence of their principles" and created a republic, they thus became citizens. With citizenship came the necessity of making political choices, and good citizens need to be educated about their society and its government to make those choices responsibly. We have seen this line of thinking in Franklin, who believed that the diffusion of knowledge through libraries helped create politically aware and democratic citizens.

The argument that democracy requires informed citizens both to make responsible decisions and to protect democracy against its enemies is almost too commonplace to dwell on, but a few representative quotes from the early years of the republic might be helpful. During the debates over the United States Constitution in the seventeen eighties, the necessity of knowledgeable republican citizens occurred in a number of places. For example, Noah Webster (signing himself "A Citizen of America") wrote in 1787 that "while property is considered as the basis of the freedom of the American yeomanry, there are other auxiliary supports; among which is the information of the people." A knowledge of government and human rights, he believed, "joined with a keen sense of liberty and a watchful jealousy, will guard our constitutions, and awaken the people to an instantaneous resistance of encroachments" (Bailyn 159). From Paris in December 1787, Thomas Jefferson wrote to James Madison expressing much the same sentiment: "Above all things I hope the education of the common people will be attended to; convinced that on their good sense we may rely with the most security for the preservation of a due degree of liberty" (213). "The Republican," writing in the *Connecticut Courant* in Hartford in January, 1787, developed the notion in slightly more depth.

> Another circumstance highly conducive to the security of liberty, is the general diffusion of knowledge among the great body of the people. The American citizens in general are by far better educated and more knowing than the people at large in other countries. . . . This is a circumstance of the highest importance to a free people. For where the great body of the citizens are ignorant, and incapable of discerning their true interests, they may be duped by artful and factious men, and led to do things destructive to their own rights and liberties. But a sensible intelligent people, who have access to the sources of information, and are capable of discerning what measures are conducive to the public welfare, will not be easily induced to act contrary to their own interests, and destroy those rights and liberties which are the foundations of public happiness. (711)

The relationship between education and republican citizens has been a constant refrain throughout the history of the United States, and indeed throughout much republican theory in general. The two main points of the relationship are that a republic must give all its citizens an equal opportunity to be educated, and that it needs those educated citizens to defend the republic against its enemies, from foreign troops to home-grown demagogues.

The republican educational logic inspired the public school movement that grew throughout the nineteenth century and the founding of numerous social agencies, including libraries. Benjamin Franklin was hardly alone in considering libraries a cornerstone of democracy. Congratulating a town in 1809 for creating a social library, Thomas Jefferson wrote that he always heard "with pleasure of institutions for the promotion of knowledge among my countrymen," because the "people of every country are the only safe guardians of their own rights," and they can guard those rights effectively only if educated. One way to achieve this education, an "extensive good at small expense," would be the "establishment of a small circulating library in every county, to consist of a few well-chosen books, to be lent to the people of the county, under such regulations as would secure their safe return in due time." Like the collection of the Library Company, such libraries would not consist of sectarian religious tracts, but would instead be very practical, "useful knowledge" being a desiderata of the Enlightenment. Thus, the books "should be such as would give them a general view of other history, and a particular view of that of their own country, a tolerable knowledge of geography, the elements of natural philosophy, of agriculture, and mechanics" (Henderson 332).

Though Jefferson himself had an enormous library larger than he could truly afford, which eventually provided the nucleus of the Library of Congress, he did not believe huge libraries were necessary to dispense knowledge effectively in a republic. Not everyone could be a scholar, but everyone needed a basic education and access to general knowledge. The foundation of small libraries of good, useful books would be sufficient, if sufficiently available to the people. Jefferson's "extensive good at small expense" foreshadows the motto of the American Library Association, coined by Melvil Dewey: "The best reading for the largest number, at the least cost." Unlike the development of universal research collections driven by the German model of higher education, the early arguments for public libraries usually focused on building collections of "the best" books. And unlike the bottom-up motivation of the Library Company, with its band of young artisans combining together to further their own self-education, public libraries as they developed in the nineteenth century were often top-down affairs, with concerned citizens founding libraries hoping to educate the mass of the people in useful, democratic ways (or to keep them docile, depending on your perspective). This was most certainly the case with the founding of the first significant public library in the United States funded primarily with public taxes, the Boston Public Library.

The Boston Public Library

The Boston Public Library was not the first publicly supported library available for the use of all the citizens in a town, but it was the most significant. Jesse Shera records three predecessors. In 1803, a Boston bookseller donated 150 books to the children of Salisbury, Connecticut, and in 1810 the citizens of Salisbury voted to give some money to support the library, thus establishing the first support of an American library from public taxes (158-59). In 1827, the town meeting of Lexington, Massachusetts "voted to establish a juvenile library and to raise sixty dollars with which to purchase books and employ a librarian" (160). A New Hampshire legislative act in 1828 gave money from a failed attempt to found a state university to the towns, with the stipulation that the money be used for "the support and maintenance of common free schools, or to other purposes of education." One town, Peterborough, interpreted the act broadly enough to consider a public library an educational institution, and founded one in 1834. "There," according to Shera, "for the first time an institution was founded by a town with the deliberate purpose of creating a free library that would be open without restriction to all classes of the community — a library supported from the beginning by public funds" (169). However, despite these early and noteworthy attempts to form truly public libraries, most historians consider the founding of the Boston Public Library to be the most significant milestone in the history of American public libraries. Shera calls the founding the "greatest single contribution to the development of the public library movement" (170), and with its founding Boston, argues Sidney Ditzion, "heavily supported by public spirit and municipal aid, seized the leadership and became a model both for general public policy and technical library practice" (13).

The Boston Public Library was slow in coming, and though established in 1854, its history could stretch back to 1841, depending on how you interpret the evidence. In that year there was a public meeting at the Mercantile Library Association to discuss the suggestion of a "French actor and ventriloquist of much talent and considerable reputation," Nicholas Marie Alexandre Vattemare, who wanted to establish an international exchange of books to cities in the United States. Boston had no public library, so Vattemare also suggested the various local libraries combine to participate in the exchange. Out of that meeting and another, later one on the subject, and following Vattemore's enthusiastic lobbying for a public library, there developed the idea of a free public library in Boston, though only with the participation and leadership of a handful of upper-class Bostonians, perhaps especially that of George Ticknor, was the library actually founded.

The prominence of the city of Boston itself and the influence building a public library there had on the rest of the country explain its historic importance. Also notable for our purposes is the long, articulate argument for founding a truly public library put forth in the founding document: "Upon the Objects to Be Attained by the Establishment of a Public Library: Report of the Trustees of the Public Library of the City of Boston 1852." The "real" reasons for founding this and other public libraries in the nineteenth century are the subject of some debate, which I will examine later, but the stated intentions of the Trustees are very clear in the Report. Public libraries extend the education provided by the free public schools to adults, both rich and poor, and such education is necessary in a republic because republican citizens must be educated and informed to make wise political decisions. A free public library will help educate citizens by providing them with good books for those already inclined to read them, and with the better popular books to elevate the taste of the library users.

The Trustees certainly admired, or claimed to admire, the free school system that had been developed in Boston. Though admitting the existence of practical problems, the "Report" nevertheless thought the system "seems perfect" and works "to give a first rate school education, at the public expense, to the entire rising generation" (Boston). The problem with the free education system is that it stops too soon. The system imparts "a knowledge of the elements of learning to all its children, but it affords them no aid in going beyond the elements," and "awakens a taste for reading, but . . . furnishes to the public nothing to be read." Perhaps most damaging to a republic that needs enlightened citizens, the educational system qualifies the young "to acquire from books the various knowledge in the arts and sciences which books contain; but it does nothing to put those books within their reach." These may seem like puzzling reasons, since in the United States today books and other means of information seem almost ubiquitous, but that ubiquity is partly the result of the benefits public libraries have provided. Prior to the Boston Public Library's founding, Boston had numerous excellent libraries, such as the Athenaeum, but these libraries were unavailable to most Boston residents. The "Report" acknowledges this, and counters the argument that multiple libraries already existed in Boston by a comparison with the public schools. Yes, many children would still be educated without them, but "all feel however that such a state of things would be a poor substitute for our system of public schools, of which it is the best feature that it is a public provision for all; affording equal advantages to poor and rich."

The very fact of republican government necessitates such public education. This theme was so entrenched by 1852 that the Trustees claimed that it "needs no argument to prove that, in a republican government, these are features of the system, quite as valuable as the direct benefit of the instruction which it imparts." Just as it needed no argument that rich and poor alike must be educated in a republic, there could "be no doubt" that "reading ought to be furnished to all, as a matter of public policy and duty, on the same principle that we furnish free education, and in fact, as a part, and a most important part, of the education of all." The link between public schools and public libraries might seem more tenuous now, especially considering the extensive programs public libraries eventually developed for children (early public libraries served adults only), but the educational function of libraries in a democratic republic should still be clear. According to the Trustees, "it has been rightly judged that, – under political, social and religious institutions like ours, – it is of paramount importance that the means of general information should be so diffused that the largest possible number of persons should be induced to read and understand questions going down to the very foundations of social order, which are constantly presenting themselves, and which we, as a people, are constantly required to decide, and do decide, either ignorantly or wisely." The arguments of the "Report" itself are not developed in depth, because the Trustees relied upon republican reasoning that by the eighteen fifties was common sense, in Boston at least, if not in the southern states.

The commonsensical republican reasoning required no argument; the connection to public libraries just needed to be made. Boston had made great strides in providing a basic education for everyone, both rich and poor, but for the "mass of the community, the public makes no provision whatever, by which the hundreds of young persons annually educated, as far as the elements of learning are concerned, at the public expense, can carry on their education and bring it to practical results by private study." The arguments for public schools were clear, and "all the reasons which exist for furnishing the means of elementary education, at the public expense, apply in an equal degree to a reasonable provision to aid and encourage the acquisition of the knowledge required to complete a preparation for active life or to perform its duties." Surely, the Trustees asserted, a "prosperous and liberal city" like Boston could "extend some reasonable amount of aid to the foundation and support of a noble public library, to which the young people of both sexes, when they leave the schools, can resort for those works which pertain to general culture, or which are needful for research into any branch of useful knowledge."

Thus, the public library was founded to serve an educational function, though it was aimed at the general public and not just scholars as other libraries in Boston often were. The library had a higher goal than merely providing good books for people to educate themselves. The Trustees also wanted to elevate the reading tastes of the people, so that they would actually want to read good books. To do that, the library must attract readers. One of the problems of the "languishing" social libraries and other libraries extant in Massachusetts was that they supplied only one copy of a book (which is still common in academic libraries), "so that if it be a new book, or one in much demand, many are obliged to wait too long for their turn to read it; so long that their desire for the book is lost, and their interest in the library diminished." Though there had been some initial debate amongst the Trustees on this matter, the "Report" advocated that popular books, or at least the "more respectable" popular books, "should be provided in such numbers, that many persons, if they desire it, can be reading the same work at the same moment, and so render the pleasant and healthy literature of the day accessible to the whole people at the only time they care for it, – that is, when it is living, fresh and new." The library should provide such popular books not because they were goods in themselves, which the Trustees did not believe, but because they hoped providing such books would "create a real desire for general reading, . . . cultivate this desire among the young, and in the families" of as many Bostonians as possible. "This taste, therefore, once excited will," the Trustees argued, "go on of itself from year to year, demanding better and better books." The advantage of this system would be the absence of any "direct control, restraint, or solicitation," because instead of telling people what to read, the library would merely cultivate a taste for reading with lesser books and then provide better reading, thus elevating the taste of the readers broadly, and "preventing at the same time, a great deal of the mischievous, poor reading now indulged in, which is bought and paid for, by offering good reading, without pay, which will be attractive." Public libraries would do more than educate citizens who wanted to read good books; they would educate citizens to *want* to read good books.

Though it persisted in various forms among librarians for, this "taste elevation theory" of the public library has been much criticized. Criticisms are fairly easy to develop. By 1901, Charles Cutter was proposing the relativist argument that would probably win most favor today. Someone had written asking him for his list of the ten best books. He wrote back asking for clarification — "Best in what? In style? In interest? In instructiveness? In suggestiveness? In power? Best for whom? For the ignorant? For children? For college graduates? For the retired scholar? For the people in general?" (Schlup 309). Cutter argued that libraries had to deal with a range of readers, and had to provide books for every level of reader. He continued that there were no best books, and that in its place any book could be the best. "There are many desirable books of very varying degrees of literacy — and other — merit, which must be provided to suit, I do not say the tastes, but the needs of the public," and that libraries catering to these needs would never be ideal libraries, but would be useful and educational (310). Cutter and many others had given up on the taste elevation theory altogether for the simple reason that it proved to be a false theory, and the public did not want its taste elevated. When public libraries provide popular books and entertainment, more people came. When they did not, more people stayed away.

The taste elevation theory has also been criticized for its "elitism" and "authoritarianism." In *The Role of the Public Library in American Life*, for example, Michael Harris argues that the entire democratic argument behind the founding of the Boston Public Library is flawed because of its elitist authoritarianism. By the eighteen forties, Boston had developed into a major destination for new immigrants, who in the opinion of the Standing Committee of the Boston Public Library thought "little of moral and intellectual culture." George Ticknor believed the massive influx of immigrants could be a problem because, in Ticknor's words, they "at no time, consisted of persons who, in general, were fitted to understand our free institutions or to be intrusted with the political power given by universal suffrage," and thus the city needed to "assimilate their masses" and accommodate them to democratic institutions, primarily through education. Harris criticizes "Ticknor's belief in the library's potential as one means of restraining the 'dangerous classes' and inhibiting the chances of unscrupulous politicians who would lead the ignorant astray," and claims this belief "explains his insistence that the public library be as popular in appeal as possible" (6). The most significant motivation behind the founding of the Boston Public Library and other libraries in the nineteenth century, Harris argues, was a fear that the masses would destabilize society, especially the immigrant masses unused to republican regimes. Any attempt to "Americanize" immigrants was "elitist" and "authoritarian," a critique developed further in Rosemary DuMont's Harris-inspired *Reform and Reaction*. The desire to elevate the reading taste of the people is just a desire to control the lower orders and prevent radical social change.

I mention this revisionist history of the founding of public libraries because it calls into question my argument that such foundings were inspired by the Enlightenment goal to educate and improve the lot of everyone, rich and poor alike. For Harris and like-minded historians, such idealistic rhetoric always masks the ambitions of the powerful to control the powerless. However, one does not have to disagree with Harris' account of George Ticknor — who did seem to be an authoritarian prig — to recognize that something as complex as the founding of a large public library could be motivated by multiple reasons, some of them perhaps contradictory. Though the 1852 "Report" goes out of its way to argue that while good books should be supplied, no one should be forced to read them, one could still argue that even thinking some books were better than others and that people should read those books is "elitist," etc. One question is whether such elitism and alleged authoritarianism are anti-democratic, and potentially counter-Enlightenment. The revisionist critique seems to imply that to be democratic in relation to books and learning means to consider all books equally good and useful and to consider all political beliefs and values worth defending, even if they are hostile or foreign to the needs of a democratic republic.

These days we would say this is a question of the value, or perhaps even the meaning, of multiculturalism, and addressing this debate in depth is out of our scope here. Harris and others (rightly in my opinion) would argue that the culture of the immigrants should be respected, but the question is, to what degree and in what areas? Let us assume that Ticknor and other upper-class Bostonians had a very conservative idea of what democracy should be; nevertheless, that does not show that they did not believe in democratic institutions. If we believe in the value of democratic institutions, then we must support those institutions, and what is more we must insist that everyone supports those institutions publicly, regardless of their private beliefs. Groups in democracies might fervently believe in fascism, but a democratic society cannot allow them to act on those beliefs. We can have a reasonable pluralism in society, but only if everyone acknowledges the authority of the public democratic institutions. What democracies cannot allow is a mere "*modus vivendi*," as the philosopher John Rawls argues, where groups abide by democratic institutions until they can be overthrown. Carrying this argument back to Ticknor, why would he not believe that immigrants from countries without democracies would need some sort of education regarding democratic institutions? How could anyone possibly believe otherwise? Is there any difference in motivation behind this belief and the practice we have in the United States of giving extensive tests on American democracy to naturalizing immigrants, tests which most natural born Americans themselves cannot pass? While some supposedly democratic criticisms of practical educational institutions are no doubt valid, we must resist the tendency to believe that all educational efforts not derived from the group being educated are inherently undemocratic. Undemocratic groups require an education in democracy.

Harris and DuMont are quite critical of the admittedly stuffy movement in nineteenth century libraries to Americanize immigrants through education, arguing that Ticknor and others merely wanted to suppress dissent and the rising ideologies of socialism and communism. Even if Ticknor and other conservatives were motivated by a fear of, say, communist demagogues convincing the undemocratic masses to revolt, or whatever the fear was, this does not undercut the fact that they did indeed seek to educate people and to provide them with the means to educate themselves throughout their lives. That the founders of the Boston Public Library were not trying to educate revolutionaries does not take away from their accomplishment. We could just as easily interpret their actions as an early stage of progressivism. For example, Jane Addams and the settlement workers in the early twentieth century wanted to "'Americanize' immigrants into the norms of their new society," but they definitely improved the lives of urban immigrants (Flanagan 37). Indeed, by the standards of the anti-immigrant movements that gained control of the American government in the nineteen twenties, George Ticknor looks like a raging liberal. Citizens of a democracy must be acculturated into democratic institutions, and criticizing this necessity because the action first arose from the conservative fear of uneducated immigrants ignores this. Even Harris is forced to admit the value public libraries had for everyone, including immigrants. "That the library's services to the immigrant had definite positive values for those able to take advantage of them cannot be denied," though he still claimed that librarians had little to do with benefit, arguing that "these positive values were the result of the immigrant's persistence and not the librarian's conscious attitude" (14). In his zeal to deny the beneficial accomplishments of anyone remotely conservative, Harris acts as if the libraries which benefitted the immigrants sprung into existence without influential citizens to found them and working librarians to run them. Regardless of whether or not an enlightened and democratic ideal was not realized in practice, it is undeniable that the Trustees of the Boston Public Library wanted to found an educational institution to allow people access to useful knowledge and give them the opportunity to educate themselves for life and citizenship, *and* that the Boston Public Library became such an institution whatever its flaws. It is also clear from the founding of the Boston Public Library to the founding of libraries throughout the century, that the most important motivating reason was the link between the public library and public education.

Carnegie Libraries

The desire to give people the means to educate and improve themselves was the avowed motivation of one of the greatest benefactors to public libraries in American history, Andrew Carnegie. Whether by fair or foul means, which is only partially relevant for the history of public libraries, Carnegie had become an enormously wealthy man by age fifty, and he spent the rest of his life spending ninety percent of his fortune on philanthropic projects. Whether he genuinely desired to provide people with public goods such as libraries, schools, and museums, or whether he merely wanted to salve his conscience or remove the taint from his fortune is a matter of dispute, then as now. The fact that Carnegie thought so carefully about how his philanthropy was to be distributed provides at least some argument for the former, because he never just threw his money at any needy cause.

Indeed, Carnegie clearly articulated his philosophy of philanthropy in two famous essays from 1889 often linked together, "The Gospel of Wealth" and "The Best Fields for Philanthropy." In "The Gospel of Wealth," Carnegie argues against the massive accumulation of wealth in a given family, and even praised the increasing prevalence of death taxes, considering them the wisest form of taxation. He wrote that, "Men who continue hoarding great sums all their lives, the proper use of which for public ends would work good to the community from which it chiefly came, should be made to feel that the community, in the form of the State, cannot thus be deprived of its proper share. By taxing estates heavily at death the State marks its condemnation of the selfish millionaire's unworthy life. As to how much should be taxed, he argued that the taxes should be graduated, from nothing on moderate estates, "and increasing rapidly as the amounts swell, until of the millionaire's hoard, as of Shylock's, at least, 'The other half / Comes to the privy coffer of the State'" (11). However, he did not believe the state should own his wealth.

Far from it. He believed that the institution of private property was necessary for the progress of modern civilization. Carnegie claimed that the "Socialist or Anarchist who seeks to overturn present conditions is to be regarded as attacking the foundation upon which civilization itself rests, for civilization took its start from the day when the capable, industrious workman said to his incompetent and lazy fellow, 'If thou dost not sow, thou shalt not reap,' and thus ended primitive Communism by separating the drones from the bees" (6). Yet he also believed that leaving huge inheritances to one's children was bad for both the children and the state. High death taxes were a way to benefit, as he saw it, both the children of the wealthy and the state, but the main benefit would be to motivate the wealthy to spend their money while they are alive, and preferably in philanthropic ways. Philanthropy done well would provide "the true antidote for the temporary unequal distribution of wealth, the reconciliation of the rich and the poor — a reign of harmony, another ideal, differing, indeed, from that of the Communist in requiring only the further evolution of existing conditions, not the total overthrow of our civilization" (12). Carnegie considered it the duty of the wealthy to give up most of their wealth for the benefit of society. They should, he said, "set an example of modest, unostentatious living, shunning display or extravagance" and "provide moderately for the legitimate wants of those dependent upon him," but after that the wealthy should consider the rest of their wealth as a trust fund which they should administer in such a way "best calculated to produce the most beneficial results for the community" (15).

Carnegie was resolutely opposed to alms-giving or indiscriminate charity, arguing that the main consideration when donating money "should be to help those who will help themselves; to provide part of the means by which those who desire to improve may do so; to give those who desire to rise the aids by which they may rise; to assist, but rarely or never to do all" (17). Much like Benjamin Franklin, Carnegie saw America as a place where people are not defined by their social hierarchies, and can better themselves through education and hard work, yet also that the opportunities to do such must be available to both the rich and the poor. Whatever its flaws — and the notion that growing labor unrest would be quelled through philanthropic endeavors by private industrialists and not organized action by the laboring classes was surely a flaw — — Carnegie's gospel of wealth and how it was to be expended nevertheless contributed significantly to the education and enrichment of many Americans through his extensive project of library building.

Why libraries? In "The Best Fields for Philanthropy" (1891), an essay aimed at the wealthy to instruct them how best to spend their money for the public good, Carnegie thought that founding a university would be the best use of money, but the second best way in general, and the best way to help communities, would be founding a public library, "provided the community will accept and maintain it as a public institution, as much a part of the city property as its public schools, and, indeed, an adjunct to these" (Carnegie 27) Note again that the public library was an adjunct to the public schools. Carnegie valued libraries specifically because of the value he had gained from one while working as a messenger boy in Pittsburgh, when "Colonel Anderson of Allegheny — a name I can never speak without feelings of devotional gratitude — opened his little library of four hundred books to boys. The working boys could take out one book every Saturday, to return it the next Saturday, and, Carnegie gushed, "no one but he who has felt it can ever know the intense longing with which the arrival of Saturday was awaited, that a new book might be had" (27). Carnegie attributed to "Colonel Anderson's precious generosity" and to "reveling in the treasures which he opened to us" a resolution that if he grew wealthy he would "establish free libraries, that other poor boys might receive opportunities similar to those for which we were indebted to that noble man" (28).

And establish free libraries he did. From 1886 until his death in 1919, Carnegie contributed $41,033,850 to the building of 1,679 library buildings in the United States, according to the figures provided by George Bobinski in his book on Carnegie libraries. This does not count the libraries he built in the United Kingdom. True to his belief that philanthropy should go only to those who wanted to help themselves, he never simply handed money to a town to build libraries. The gifts were for the buildings alone, and were for a "stipulated amount if the city provided a suitable site for the building and agreed by a resolution of its council to support a public library annually at a cost of no less than 10 percent of the total sum contributed" (Bobinski 40). Carnegie received criticism for this firm rule throughout the era of his library philanthropy and beyond, but the gift of a free building spurred most of the communities to actually support public libraries in places that before had inadequate or nonexistent facilities. The Carnegie library building campaign provided a major incentive for the building of hundreds of public libraries, often in small towns, and it was motivated by the desire to spread the benefits of education to all who wanted to educate themselves.

Undoubtedly, this generosity is vulnerable to the same criticisms Harris leveled against Ticknor and the founding of the Boston Public Library. Indeed, Harris criticizes Carnegie and his fellow philanthropists for considering "the library a wise investment in order, stability, and sound economic growth," as if order, stability, and economic growth benefit the wealthy alone. Wealthy philanthropic efforts just "further encouraged [librarians] in their conservative, authoritarian, and elitist stance," he claims (15). Carnegie supposedly "reinforced their authoritarianism" because he said that "'the result of knowledge [gleaned from libraries] is to make men not violent revolutionists, but cautious evolutionists; not destroyers, but careful improvers,'" which Harris considers ample condemnation of Carnegie. Harris also considers it a criticism of libraries that they best serve those who want to use them, rather than acting as some sort of revolutionary agency, though he never articulates exactly how a municipal institution that at the time was primarily a means of distributing books to people could take on an active revolutionary role, or why anyone would support it if it did. Harris' detailed critique of Carnegie's motivation smacks of his own elitism, ironically enough. Carnegie believed that libraries could help provide social stability, but in doing so "assumed that the common man, if properly motivated and rewarded, could learn" (15). However, Harris argues that "this faith in the common man's capacity to learn was exaggerated," and that "a naive and generally unfounded belief in the average American's interest in cultural matters led men like Carnegie to scrutinize insistently the statistical records of public libraries seeking evidence of a general elevation of the masses." In his urge to condemn such library philanthropy, Harris confuses capacity with interest. However, the lack of general interest in the educational mission of public libraries continued to be a point of debate for decades to come as the public library movement grew in the United States.

Efforts of the American Library Association

From its founding in 1876, the American Library Association has often lead the movement to found and support public libraries in the United States, and its rhetoric from the earliest days into the twentieth century often echoes the justifications of public libraries that we have seen from Benjamin Franklin to Andrew Carnegie: the most important role of public libraries is to educate the people and improve their lives.

In the first issue of the *Library Journal* in 1876, Melvil Dewey explicitly made the connection between libraries and education. "Our leading educators," he writes, "have come to recognize the library as sharing with the school the education of the people" (Dewey 6). Echoing the 1852 "Report" of the Boston Public Library Trustees, he claims that while the "school teaches them to read; the library must supply them with reading which shall serve to educate, and so it is that we are forced to divide popular education into two parts of almost equal importance and deserving equal attention: the free school and the free library." Twenty-five years had done nothing to change the justification for public libraries, actually forty-five years if we remember the early Peterborough public library. The justification remained consistent because the educational mission of public libraries proved the most persuasive reason to fund them through taxation, even well into the twentieth century.

By Dewey's time, the most significant change was the elevation in status of the librarian, or rather the attempt by librarians — through professional organizations like the ALA itself — to elevate their status. If public libraries are of a kind with public schools, then public librarians must be like public school teachers, that is, educators, but of adults instead of children. (We should remember that public libraries were aimed at adults only until the eighteen nineties, when services to children started to develop.) Dewey believed that with hard work by librarians people would begin to consider the public library in the same category as the public school, and wrote that the "time *was* when a library was very like a museum, and a librarian was a mouser in musty books, and visitors looked with curious eyes at ancient tomes and manuscripts. The time *is* when a library is a school, and the librarian is in the highest sense a teacher" (Schlup 42). However, while librarians communicating amongst themselves in the organs of professional associations wrote about their own professional development, ALA propaganda aimed at founding libraries focused strictly on the library and its educational benefit, not the increasingly professional and specially trained skills of librarians.

A good example of ALA efforts to promote the founding of public libraries is the small book, *Why Do We Need a Public Library?: Material for a Library Campaign*, that appeared in several editions during the first decade of the twentieth century. It was designed to give people interested in founding public libraries in their community a wealth of material to convince their fellow citizens to establish a library, including press releases and suggested strategies of persuasion.

The 1902 edition begins with "What a Library Does for a Country Town," which is billed a "Connecticut Public Library Document, 1895." The 1910 edition (from which I am quoting) attributes the piece to Caroline M. Hewins, an important public library leader of the era and librarian for fifty years at what is now the Hartford (CT) Public Library. The benefits of the library to a country town are many, but not varied:

1. It keeps boys at home in the evening by giving them well-written stories of adventure.
2. It gives teachers and pupils interesting books to aid their school work in history and geography, and makes better citizens of them by enlarging their knowledge of their country and its growth.
3. It provides books on the care of children and animals, cookery and housekeeping, building and gardening, and teaches young readers how to make simple dynamos, telephones and other machines.
4. It helps clubs that are studying history, literature or life in other countries, and throws light upon Sunday school lessons.
5. It furnishes books of selections for reading aloud, suggestions for entertainments and home amusements, and hints on correct speech and good manners.
6. It teaches the names and habits of the plants, birds and insects of the neighborhood, and the differences in soil and rock.

7. It tells the story of the town from its settlement, and keeps a record of all important events in its history.
8. It offers pleasant and wholesome stories to readers of all ages. (Chalmers 5-6)

Hewins' list of the benefits a public library brings to a country town is unusual only in that it begins by touting something other than the educational benefits of the library. Other than keeping boys out of trouble by providing them with well written stories and offering "pleasant and wholesome stories" to all readers, the rest of the list extols the educational virtues of the library. It aids in school work and Sunday school lessons, helps to create better educated citizens, teaches about this country as well as other countries, and brings the wealth of scientific knowledge accumulated since the Enlightenment to the town. Not just theoretical knowledge, either, but practical knowledge of geology and mechanics, just the sort of useful knowledge Benjamin Franklin had to organize his own social library to acquire. As with the founding intentions of the Boston Public Library, even the fiction was to be well written and wholesome, because the public library was not intended to be a receptacle of mere entertainment for the masses, but only the best reading. The public library may also entertain, but its primary mission was to educate, elevate, and inspire.

By 1910, *Why Do We Need a Public Library?* included other checklists as well. It now began with Frederick Morgan Crunden, another significant library leader and the longtime librarian who modernized and improved the St. Louis Public Library. He tells us "What a Public Library Does for a Community":

1. It doubles the value of the education the child receives in school, and, best of all, imparts a desire for knowledge which serves as an incentive to continue his education after leaving school; and, having furnished the incentive, it further supplies the means for a life-long continuance of education.
2. It provides for the education of adults who have lacked, or failed to make use of, early opportunities.
3. It furnishes information to teachers, ministers, journalists, physicians, legislators, all persons upon whose work depend the intellectual, moral, sanitary and political welfare and advancement of the people.
4. It furnishes books and periodicals for the technical instruction and information of mechanics, artisans, manufacturers, engineers and all others whose work requires technical knowledge — of all persons upon whom depends the industrial progress of the city.
5. It is of incalculable benefit to the city by affording to thousands the highest and purest entertainment, and thus lessening crime and disorder.
6. It makes the city a more desirable place of residence, and thus retains the best citizens and attracts others of the same character.
7. More than any other agency, it elevates the general standard of intelligence throughout the great body of the community, upon which its material prosperity, as well as its moral and political well-being, must depend. Finally, the public library includes potentially all other means of social betterment. A library is a living organism, having within itself the capacity of infinite growth and reproduction. It may found a dozen museums and hospitals, kindle the train

of thought that produces beneficent inventions, and inspire to noble deeds of every kind, all the while imparting intelligence and inculcating industry, thrift, morality, public spirit and all those qualities that constitute the wealth and well-being of a community. (Chalmers 4-5)

Crunden's list begins with the familiar rhetoric of the 1852 Boston "Report": the library continues the people's education after they leave school, but his list is even more heavily devoted to educational purposes than Hewins' list. Physicians, legislators, mechanics, and engineers all have something to learn at the public library. Despite the educational emphasis, Crunden expands the mission and possibility of the public library well beyond Hewins and many other librarians claimed for it. Not only does providing the "highest and purest entertainment" reduce crime — presumably because potential criminals would either be too busy reading great books to commit crimes, or because great books would elevate them to the point where they would learn the folly of their ways — but the public library has an economic benefit as well by making the city a more desirable place to live. By point seven, one gets the idea that a city really needs nothing but a public library, and from that all good things flow, since a library has "within itself the capacity of infinite growth and reproduction." The implication is that one could place a library and a few hundred people in the middle of the wilderness, and the highest civilization would emerge.

After we discover what the library can do for a community and for a country town, we find out more about "What a Library Does for a Town" from "A.W. in New York Libraries" (the New York Inspector of Schools in 1909, Asa Wynkoop). For a town, a public library:

1. Completes its educational equipment, carrying on and giving permanent value to the work of the schools.
2. Gives the children of all classes a chance to know and love the best in literature. Without the public library such a chance is limited to the very few.
3. Minimizes the sale and reading of vicious literature in the community, thus promoting mental and moral health.
4. Effects a great saving in money to every reader in the community. The library is the application of common sense to the problem of supply and demand. Through it every reader in the town can secure at a given cost from 100 to 1000 times the material for reading or study that he could secure by acting individually.
5. Appealing to all classes, sects and degrees of intelligence, it is a strong unifying factor in the life of a town.
6. The library is the one thing in which every town, however poor or isolated, can have something as good and inspiring as the greatest city can offer. Neither Boston nor New York can provide better books to its readers than the humblest town library can easily own and supply.
7. Slowly but inevitably raises the intellectual tone of a place.
8. Adds to the material value of property. Real estate agents in the suburbs of large cities never fail to advertise the presence of a library, if there be one, as giving added value to the lots or houses they have for sale.

The list is still overwhelmingly focused on the educational benefit of public libraries, from allowing people to continue their education after their formal schooling has ended to raising the "intellectual tone" of the town. Though he does not go so far as Crunden, Wynkoop's list of library virtues does extend past education to general political, moral, and economic improvement in a town. All classes, the rich and the poor, will benefit from the public library, and indeed the public library will unify the classes — the public library as utopia. Property values will rise and citizens will save money, providing important — though not Enlightenment-related — economic justifications for public libraries. Point six pushes the bounds of plausibility, but undoubtedly without a public library a poor and isolated town at the time would have had almost no access to good books, or any books.

By the mid-nineteen twenties, faith in the educational mission of the public library began to wane, even among librarians. One indication is the attempt by the American Library Association to delineate possible ways in which public libraries could support the steadily growing adult education movement that had emerged in Europe and spread into America. In 1924, the ALA commissioned a group to study the possibilities, and in 1926 the ALA Commission on the Library and Adult Education published *Libraries and Adult Education*. After working through a number of definitions of "adult education," the Commission noted that most library work has nothing to do with educating adults by any of those definitions. Indeed, the "purely recreational features" and "the ordinary processes of obtaining and furnishing information" were excluded from the usual definitions of "adult education," though "the latter constitute an essential service in support of adult education." The contrast between the high educational tone of the earlier generation of librarians and the thoughts of the Commission are captured nicely as the Commission writes that, "after all possible limitations have been made, however, there are certain library services that are acknowledged to be distinctly educational" (17). Frederick Crunden would have been glad to hear it. The Commission mentioned several possibilities for librarians to get involved with the work of adult education, including arousing more interest in reading among the young to develop lifelong reading habits, supplying easily readable books for adults who never developed the reading habit, and the development of better central lending services so that smaller and poorer libraries would actually be able to supply good books for adult education efforts. It turns out that Asa Wynkoop was wrong; humble libraries cannot supply the same quality of books as those in large cities.

Despite the problems surrounding adult education, the American Library Association still promoted the educational mission of public libraries above all else. For example, the ALA "National Plan for Libraries" of 1934 stated that libraries are to acquire and organize books and promote their use. This could sound merely technical, rather than educational, but books and their promotion were to give people the "opportunity and encouragement"

- to educate themselves continuously;
- to aid in the advancement of knowledge;
- to improve their capacity for appreciation and production in cultural fields;
- to improve their ability to participate usefully in activities in which they are involved as citizens;
- to equip themselves, and keep themselves equipped, for efficient activity in useful occupations and practical affairs;
- to keep abreast of progress in the sciences and other fields of knowledge'

- to maintain the precious heritage of freedom of expression and a constructively critical attitude toward all public issues;
- to make such use of leisure time as will promote personal happiness and social well-being." (quoted in Williams 47)

This list could have provided the intellectual foundations of the Library Company of Philadelphia, and it shows that in times of crisis, or often enough in times of possible funding, librarians fall back on the mission originally articulated for public libraries: to educate the citizens of a democracy for better lives and improved citizenship.

Despite the retreat into educational defenses, the public library support of the adult education movement did not live up to its greatest potential. In *The Public Library: a People's University*, a 1938 study funded by the Carnegie Corporation and published by the American Association of Adult Education, economist Alvin Saunders Johnson strongly criticized the insufficient efforts of public libraries to support the adult education movement. Some problems were outside the control of librarians. Johnson noted that libraries were always poorly funded, quick to get their budgets slashed in recessions, and slow to get them restored in better times, which is still true today. Poor budgets affect both the quantity of books and staff, and overworked librarians were understandably loath to add adult education promotion to their portfolios. However, some problems were endemic to the profession. Library schools, he wrote, were devoted to "pure librarianship, the impartial custodianship and administration of books" (76), which precludes an interest in books as a means of education. Librarians were often simply technicians, who had "been educated to regard themselves as custodians and administrators of books, books in general, whether or not educational and educationally employed" (61). Johnson considered the general quality of librarians suspect as well, claiming that the "profession is notoriously underpaid but secure, and many persons strike for it as for other professions, for no better reason than lack of other opportunities" (76).

Johnson's most serious criticism of the educational efforts of librarians focuses on the way in which librarians had begun to quantify their popularity, a decided shift from the high-minded rhetoric of earlier days. Because librarians were technicians supplying books rather than educators, the quantity of circulation trumped the quality of the product circulated. Circulation was more important to the librarian that supporting adult education. Johnson argued that, "if adult educational work will increase the circulation of books, at the same time raising the quality of the circulation, all librarians will regard this as related to their proper function. But if adult education should involve changes in operations that resulted in a reduction of circulation, most librarians would regard this with misgivings" (61). Addressing the possible counter-argument that public libraries exist to serve the public and give them the books they want, rather than what books the librarians would think best (a philosophy of librarianship at odds with that which earlier generations used to promote the founding of public libraries), Johnson says the argument "is exactly the one used by a department store head to justify him in offering for sale good merchandise, vulgar merchandise, merchandise that can float only on the folly of the purchaser." However, department stores exist simply to make money, not supply a public service, and he questions "whether the library, which exists not to make money but to perform a public service, does not require another argument for its book selection and circulation policy" (70). For Johnson, as for many critics before and since, the further public libraries strayed from an educational function, the less of a public service they provided. Even if we accept that "giving the public what it wants" still provides some sort of public service, it is not an educational service as such.

The post-war *National Plan for Public Library Service*, published by the ALA in 1948, seemed to agree. It proposed an ambitious, expensive, and to some extent eventually achieved "nation-wide minimum standard of service and support below which no library should fall" (160), calling for building libraries, supporting cooperative services, and participation by government at the local, state, and national level. While many excellent libraries existed, nationally libraries had no such standard, and in many parts of the country were in sorry shape indeed. Lowell Martin, writing the first chapter on the "potential of the American public library" extolled the educational potentials of the public library in the great tradition from Ticknor on forward. For Martin, the two major objectives of public libraries, out of which lesser goals derived, are "to promote enlightened citizenship and to enrich personal life. They have to do with the twin pillars of the American way, the democratic process of group life, and the sanctity and dignity of the individual person" (16). (The long-lived and productive Martin remained consistent, and his 1998 history of American public libraries entitled *Enrichment* makes much the same argument.)

Martin emphasized the educational mission of public libraries over any other, and argued that librarians would be most effective if they had a sense of purpose regarding that mission. A library must have "an explicit concept of improvements which it aims to foster in its constituents," and regardless of how large it is, "an agency which has not adopted objectives for removing ignorance, intolerance, and insensibility is not an educational institution but a supply source for whoever decides to make demands upon it." Echoing Johnson, but with less bite, Martin compares a library that merely provides whatever its patrons want with commercial agencies. By following rather than leading their patrons, he argues, libraries find themselves "disregarded by the very citizens they aspire to serve. Libraries furnish recreational reading materials, but they are not the prime source for such materials; they provide educational services, but they are not the major center of such services; they disseminate information, but they are not the main source of community intelligence. For lack of clear-cut objectives some public libraries dissipate rich resources without appreciable effect" (12). He admits that libraries often have an implicit sense of purpose, since they were not (at least then) "filled with comic books, confession magazines, and sex stories," but this sense of purpose is vague and inarticulate.

Martin asserts that developing a sense of purpose does not involve "championing strange doctrines" or "taking sides in controversial issues," because the purpose would have to be limited by the values of the community, and "no community would long endure a . . . library which undermined accepted notions of the individual and the state" (12). Thus, while the library has a political charge to educate citizens, it is restricted by the prevailing political notions in a community. This is somewhat inconsistent with the idea that an educational agency would be unworthy of the name if it did not seek to remove ignorance and intolerance. The existence of many oppressed and discriminated-against portions of the population then and today demands challenging acceptable intolerance in many communities, and indeed taking sides on controversial issues. However, that side-taking will always be on the side of reason, freedom, education, and tolerance. Martin mitigates this inconsistency somewhat by claiming that educating citizens is not subversive, and that the "benefits at this moment of seven thousand public libraries devoting themselves to the dissemination of comprehensive, unbiased, forceful information about atomic energy, or about world organization for peace, would be invaluable" (13). Martin could state even more forcefully the educational role of book selection in libraries. The current dominant belief among public librarians requires libraries to provide a neutral and balanced collection on controversial issues, which assumes that every side of an issue is worth representing. Sometimes libraries are criticized from the right for having "unbalanced" collections. For example, an anti-homosexual organization called Americans for Truth about Homosexuality claimed in 2006 that it was launching a "'Library Fairness Project' to correct the severe pro-homosexual book bias in local library collections nationwide" (Americans). (Though as far as I can tell, the press release announcing the intention is the only manifestation of the "Library Fairness Project.") The organization wants to help citizens request "local libraries to have balanced collections on homosexuality," which would "include books by former homosexuals ('ex-gays') — a subject despised by liberal, pro-gay activists intent on hiding the truth that many men and women have left that sinful lifestyle." Rather than being intent on "hiding the truth," it is just as likely that librarians refuse to spend money on marginal right-wing material unless it is specifically requested. Despite the claims to neutrality, this is what one would expect of a social agency governed by the spirit of the Enlightenment, and dedicated to reason and individual freedom rather than sectarian religious views of homosexuality.

Though today the American Library Association is more likely to promote the provision of information as the mission of public libraries, it should be clear that for several decades, despite the failures, problems, and criticisms of public libraries as educational institutions, it continued to hearken back to the foundational rhetoric of public libraries as agencies of education and enlightenment in a democracy.

The Purpose of Public Libraries

It should be clear from the brief history presented here that public libraries began as instruments of enlightenment, hoping to spread knowledge and culture broadly to the people, who as free citizens of a democratic republic required access to that knowledge and culture to live fuller lives and to become better citizens. The question is whether that original motivation still has any place in a philosophy of public libraries. The course of the twentieth century proved that no matter how high the purpose or grand the rhetoric of the public library movement, people just did not use public libraries *en masse*, and those that did use public libraries were primarily interested in entertainment. As a result, public libraries shifted from instruments of enlightenment to information and entertainment centers, and librarians shifted from purveyors of education to neutral providers of that information and entertainment. Instead of enlightenment and education, the goal eventually became to get as many people using libraries as possible, regardless of whether that use had anything to do with the traditional purposes of the public library. Whatever the library should be, it should first be *popular*, because without that popularity public libraries would get even less funding than they already did. Thus, public libraries offered an increasing range of services, but lost a strong sense of purpose. People have been debating the purpose of public libraries since their inception, and I am not going to delve deeply into the debate here. However, if the past of the public library has anything to say about the future, then the history presented here might have something to offer that debate.

The belief that public libraries had somehow failed in their initial mission to educate the people existed at least as early as the nineteen thirties. In her 1934 essay on "The Democratic Function of Public Libraries," Grace O. Kelley argued that public libraries seem "not to have been altogether a true part of the social process" and occupied a niche of their own. "One looks in vain," she writes, "in histories of culture and education for studies of the modern library as an active force which is making its impress upon the social fabric." (I find that true even today, having scoured numerous histories for any mention of libraries.) Instead of fulfilling the educational mission that initially motivated the foundation of public libraries, they have continued "to function largely on [their] original indefinite ideals and, in a sense, to let the modern world go by" (11). One problem was the increasing specialization of knowledge, which needed to be disseminated somehow in popular form so that interested readers could digest it. A "clear" function of public libraries would be the dissemination of specialized knowledge to general readers, and "forward-looking librarians" needed to find books understandable by those general readers. According to Kelley, "we can have faith to believe that the intelligent reading of worth-while books on important matters that are of mutual interest both to the reader and to the author will result gradually in a clearer understanding of the changing concepts of society and all of its problems," and that this understanding "will lead to a more effective and enlightened control over social conditions, increase the probability of happier and more successful living, and in this way justify the vision of democracy" (15). Faith, the Epistle to the Hebrews tells us, is "the assurance of things hoped for, the conviction of things not seen," and that democratic faith remains strong despite so much contrary evidence.

One of the most vigorous critics of the devolution of the public library's educational mission is Patrick Williams, writing fifty years after Kelley but maintaining the same faith in the educational mission of the public library. In *The American Public Library and the Problem of Purpose*, Williams documents that devolution in great detail, showing the anxious debates among librarians over the decades as it became clearer that the public library could never serve the public in the grand educational manner librarians in the nineteenth century had hoped, and mostly because the public was not interested. Despite the failure of the original mission, Williams still concludes that education in some sense should once again be highlighted as the purpose of the public library. Restoring the "identity of the public library as an institution of informal self-education" would mean returning "to what made the library grow, develop, and earn the respect and support of the public in the first place," and allowing the library to focus on "the only task of importance that it ever performed, providing education for those who seek it." Williams' solution to the "problem of purpose" is cold and somewhat quixotic. Providing education for those who seek it is definitely not the same thing as being "an instrument of self-education for the masses," and while restoring the identity of the library as an educational institution, librarians "must do so without the vision that inspired their predecessors, the vision of educating the masses." The only advantage contemporary librarians would have is that "their educational task will not be doomed to be repeated and inevitable failure" (137), which does not strike me as much of an advantage. Why bother restoring an identity that apparently leads only to failure? After a worthwhile analysis and discussion of that repeated and inevitable failure, his conclusion seems to me to provide very little inspiration for librarians to revitalize the mission of public libraries as educational institutions.

In their essay "Democratic Ideals and the American Public Library," Arthur Hafner and Jennifer Sterling-Folker reemphasize the educational mission of the public library, but in what, to me at least, seems a stronger and more inspirational manner. They criticize the shift toward trying to make libraries popular with little regard to purpose or mission. However, they do understand the reasons behind that shift, as librarians grew disillusioned that "based on the statistical evidence, the public library does not appear to be an important source of information for the American public" (20). Only a small percentage of the public uses public libraries for educational purposes, as has been the case from the very beginning of public libraries in America. However, they argue, popularity should not be confused with importance or necessity, and they criticize marketing public libraries as popular entertainment centers with "no justification made for the public library's existence on historical, social, or moral grounds and no recognition that libraries are and must continue to be intimately bound to their societal contexts to be meaningful agencies" (24), echoing the criticisms of Alvin Saunders Johnson from the nineteen thirties. They argue that, historically, there is no connection between the popularity and use of public libraries and the public's willingness to fund them. Successful public library campaigns emphasize the educational mission of the public library, and people seem to like the idea of the public library even if they themselves make no use of it (32). After rehearsing the arguments about the necessity of access to education in a democracy that I covered earlier, Hafner and Sterling-Folker make the case that libraries should reaffirm their democratic purpose, arguing that "statistics by themselves are no substitute for the library's purpose," and that "the reaction of the American public to the popularization of the public library seems to indicate that people would rather have the library fulfill its traditional democratic function with low usage numbers than have it compete with commercial entertainment enterprises for higher usage numbers" (35).

Hafner and Sterling-Folker make a strong case for the continued importance of public libraries for citizens in a democracy. In democracies, those citizens are of singular importance in themselves and *as* citizens. Thus, their own cultivation and self-realization as well as their education on topics relevant to political decisions are also important. However, despite having equal political rights, people are not equal in their means and opportunities, and therefore democratic institutions emerge to equalize the opportunities for citizens and give them the means of cultivation and education. (Or so the theory goes.) "To ensure the individual's development," they argue, democratic societies must provide some agency to make all knowledge available equally to all citizens, and the public library is that agency, and it is the only agency that does so for the public good. "The public library is the only agency in American society that makes knowledge, ideas, and information freely available to all citizens," and "as such it is the only agency in American society whose sole function is to guard against the tyrannies of ignorance and conformity" (18). Because of this, it is especially important for public libraries to resist commercialization, of becoming merely a public way of getting private entertainment.

The control of knowledge "either by the few over the many or by the majority over the minority" results in "political and social tyranny," and the public library is the only storehouse of knowledge that can combat this control for the majority of people (25). Libraries should resist the logic of the marketplace, the idea that unless everyone wants it, nobody gets it. Haffner and Sterling-Folker argue that the market "selects and promotes only those opinions and views that are profitable," and therefore "does not protect new ideas and the individual's right to information and knowledge." For those without access to academic libraries, only public libraries can defend that right, but by becoming merely purveyors of popular entertainment libraries are in danger of "promoting the very conformity and sameness that they, as symbols of our highest political ideals, should be fighting against" (26). The counter-argument that popular entertainment is what the people want, and libraries should mostly be in the business of providing what people want, evades this line of argument without refuting it.

The popularization argument pretends to be neutral and value-free, but no method is value-free. If popularity is the justification for public library collections, rather than some political or moral purpose, then only the most profitable knowledge and information will be available. "The public library remains the only source for the pursuit of independent thought, critical attitudes, and in-depth information," and the "fact that the majority of Americans do not wish to pursue independent thought on a daily basis does not undercut the tremendous social value of providing for the pursuit of knowledge for those who want it," because "the pursuit of knowledge and self-enlightenment lies at the heart of our democracy" (27). In other words, public libraries supplying the best information are crucial for democracies, *even if* no one uses those libraries, whereas public libraries supplying merely the most popular materials have chosen the default value that whatever information makes the most money is the best information, period.

Williams was writing in the 1980s, and Hafner and Sterling-Folker in the 1990s. Since then, the most significant development that could challenge their arguments is the rise of the Internet. Wade through public comments about libraries on blogs, news articles, and other forums, and inevitably you will find someone claiming that public libraries are now irrelevant because all the information people need is available through the Internet. Some of the pro-public library propaganda implicitly accepts this as a legitimate talking point, because it often mentions the fact that some thirty percent of Americans would have no access to the Internet without public libraries, thus implying that Internet access itself is a justification for funding libraries.

However, the argument itself is flawed, because current, in-depth information on most topics is just not freely available through the Internet. Pre-1923 books are widely available through Project Gutenberg and other means, but information that is currently in copyright (i.e., published after 1923) is not. The Internet is awash in free information, and even more free misinformation, but if someone wanted to read a book-length treatment, or even better multiple book-length treatments of most topics, the choice would either be to pay for the information or find it in a library. This even includes much publicly funded information, since the results of a significant amount of research funded by the federal government ends up in scholarly journals published by commercial publishers. Hafner and Sterling-Folker argue that "the public library assists in the realization and reinforcement of a democratic society by being that society's storehouse of *all* knowledge and accessible to every citizen" [my italics] (18). I believe this is in fact the ultimate goal of both academic and public libraries, to make all knowledge accessible to every citizen, a universal library accessible to all, but public libraries have not come as close to achieving this goal for various reasons, mostly having to do with mission, funding, and public disinterest. Academic libraries have more or less achieved this goal for published information, but only for the relative few who are actively affiliated with a college or university. For the majority, such a universal library does not exist. While it is true that the vast majority of people have no interest in examining issues in depth, and thus no need for a universal library, the absence of such a library nevertheless goes against the democratic ideal to provide citizens with the means to cultivate and educate themselves regardless of their means. Commercial logic must be reversed for a universal library: if somebody wants it, everybody gets it.

As we will see in the next chapter, a universal library has been a dream since the Library of Alexandria, and especially since the Enlightenment some have attempted to make that dream a reality in the modern world. Only with the fulfillment of that dream would America achieve the possibility for the enlightenment of all citizens, rich and poor alike.

CHAPTER IV

Universal Libraries: Dream and Reality

THE ENLIGHTENMENT inspired more than just actual academic and public libraries. It also inspired the dream of a universal library. The goal of the Universal Library as I interpret it is to collect, organize, and make accessible the world's knowledge for the enlightenment of those who use the library. The ultimate goal of a universal library would be for everyone in the world to be able to find and access every human document or form of information ever created any time from any place. The dream of a universal library is as old as the Library at Alexandria and as new as Google, and it has yet to be achieved. In ancient times, the problem was collecting every existing document, in modern times finding the ones we want in the unimaginably enormous information universe. It ranges from actual attempts to collect every book available to efforts to scale universal knowledge to a manageable representation. The Library that can be created is not the

Universal Library, as Lao Tzu might have said had he been a librarian, but the dream of a universal library tempts us still. All libraries are an approximation of that dream. A Universal Library accessible to all would be the culmination of the Enlightenment in the domain of information.

The Library at Alexandria

The original universal library was no dream of the Enlightenment, but it is worth examining for comparison. The famous Library at Alexandria is the one library of the ancient world that everyone seems to have heard of, and for good reason. Even in ancient times, the Library was legendary for having the largest collection of scrolls in the world. Though not the only great library or the first, over time its collection and the scholarly contributions to culture its collection allowed gave it the reputation it deserved. It was the first Universal Library.

We might see it from a distance of centuries as something of a noble dream, and it was exactly that, a *noble* dream, insomuch as the Library was founded for the greater glory and control of the ruling family of Egypt, the Ptolomies. When Alexander the Great died in 323 BC, his empire was eventually divided into three sections, each ruled by one of the leading groups of his generals. Antigonids controlled Greece, Seleucids controlled much of Asia Minor, and the Ptolemies controlled Egypt and had their capital at Alexandria (Casson 32). The Ptolomies ruled from Alexander's death until the death of Cleopatra in 30 BC, though the Library they founded and supported lasted several more generations. They were a learned family, and as rulers fared well in the division of Alexander's empire. Egypt was the richest of the three divisions, with ample grain to export to the rest of the world.

Egypt also had a monopoly on the most popular writing material in the ancient world — papyrus. The papyrus plant grew abundantly in the Nile River delta. To make papyrus, the pith of the papyrus plant was cut into strips about a foot and a half long. Moistened strips were laid in rows, then columns crossing the rows, which were then dried under pressure and rubbed smooth to create a fragile but sufficient writing surface. These pieces were sewn together to create the scrolls perhaps twenty sheets long that served the ancients as books. A scroll might contain several short "books," or a long "book" such as Homer's *Iliad* or *Odyssey* might fill several scrolls. Every "book" in every scroll had to be handwritten by a scribe with a quill pen and might take hundreds of hours to create. At its height, the Library at Alexandria contained close to half a million scrolls.

The Library's collection development policy (to use some librarian jargon) was comprehensive. *Everything* was to be collected. The Ptolomies spoke Greek, so the focus first of all was on collecting every bit of Greek writing. In addition, the Library collected translations of major works from other languages into Greek. Relatively little ancient Greek literature has survived, but at one point every work of any importance was collected in one place, and, if the Library was like research libraries today, much that proved unimportant. The Library at Alexandria was the first deliberately universal library, intended to collect everything into one place. Such a library was inconceivable again for several hundred years, and by the time thoughts turned again to the universal library concept, no single library could contain the written record.

When we consider the size and scope of the Library, two questions come to mind: Why, and how? What purpose could such a library serve, and how could such a collection possibly be gathered in one place? As with so many great endeavors, we could answer *power* and *money*.

The Library served many purposes. Its greatness brought glory to the Ptolemies, so much so that they were fiercely jealous of any similar ventures. For example, the greatest rival to the Library of Alexandria was the Library at Pergamum, said at one point to contain 200,000 scrolls (which were supposedly later given to the Library at Alexandria as a wedding present from Marc Antony to Cleopatra). Because of this jealous rivalry, the Ptolemies stopped exporting papyrus to Pergamum so that the library there could not build its collection. This led, so the story goes, to the development of parchment at Pergamum as an alternative writing material.

The Ptolomies were also learned, and wanted to support research and scholarship, which itself brought more learned scholars to Alexandria and increased its power. First, Ptolemy I founded the Museum. Today, we think of museums as places that collect art or historical objects, but originally a museum was a temple to the Muses and the arts they represent: epic poetry, lyric poetry, choral poetry, tragedy, comedy, music, dance, history, and astronomy. The Museum hosted scholars and writers whom Ptolemy fed, housed, and appointed for life. The Library was then founded to support the work of these scholars.

The work was impressive. Zenodotus, the first director of the library, is the first person known to use alphabetical organization; he also edited the first standard edition of Homer's works. Aristophanes and Aristarchus edited standard editions of other poets, and Aristarchus also wrote numerous commentaries on poetry. Philitas produced the first lexicons and glossaries of rare words in Greek. Didymus also produced numerous commentaries and glossaries. Dionysius Thrax wrote the first grammar book. Another of the library directors, Callimachus, produced a comprehensive bibliography of Greek writing, the "Pinakes" ("Tables"), which probably served as a catalog for the works in the Library. (Its full title was *Tables of Persons Eminent in Every Branch of Learning together with a List of Their Writings*.) As Lionel Casson notes in *Libraries in the Ancient World*, "the first two phases of Alexandrian scholarship had produced such indispensible tools of scholarship as the authoritative text edition, the commentary, the glossary; the last phase added one more — the grammar" (45).

And how did the Ptolemies amass such an enormous collection of scrolls? They sent out purchasing agents with orders to buy everything possible. They borrowed and copied scrolls from other libraries. They searched ships that docked at Alexandria, confiscated any scrolls, copied them, and returned the *copies* to the ship. These scrolls, fittingly enough, became part of the "ship collection." Ptolemy III was desperate to get his hands on the official versions of the great plays of Sophocles, Euripides, and Aeschylus kept in Athens. The Athenians agreed to loan them to be copied, but only for a huge monetary deposit. Ptolemy left a deposit, borrowed the scrolls, had copies made, and then — as with the ships — returned the copies to Athens, forfeiting the deposit (35). Collectors of all sorts will notice the mania of the Ptolemies, but with vast wealth and enormous power this mania created the greatest library in the ancient world.

Though there were other great libraries in the ancient world — at Pergamum and Ephesus, for example — the Library at Alexandria was the only one to fulfill the ultimate goals of a *universal* library: a comprehensive, accessible collection. This sets it apart not only from the ancient Greek libraries, but also from ancient libraries before or after the Library at Alexandria. No previous library combined a comprehensive collection with accessibility (at least to qualified scholars if not to everyone).

For example, one of the earliest known libraries was at Hattasus (in modern-day Turkey), the capital of the Hittite empire from about 1700-1200 BC. Ashurbanipal, King of Assyria from 668-627 BC, also founded a library, and is the first named person to do so. However, these libraries, however large they may have been, were royal libraries in the strictest sense — created for the use of kings and the priests who worked to maintain the king's power. The goal was nothing so lofty as a comprehensive collection of all known writing or the creation of scholarship and learning.

Libraries in ancient Rome were often publicly available, and frequently part of the popular Roman bathhouses, but they were hardly comprehensive. In early years, only wealthy aristocrats owned libraries, and scholars like Cicero got access to books through the libraries of their friends. But even later, as there were royal libraries and public libraries, there was no central library building a comprehensive collection of all Latin writing that we know of. Although Casson, for example, claims that "we can be certain that everything in the language of value was to be found there. Rome's libraries together did for Latin what Alexandria's single great library did for Greek," even he has to admit that "the information available enables us to cite but a few random titles that were among the holdings of the Latin chambers in Rome's libraries" (102). Without sufficient evidence, we can only make a reasonable judgment this was true. Even if it is true, however, libraries scattered throughout a city — in public and private hands — could never provide the comprehensive, organized, and thus accessible collection of all writing that would qualify as a universal library. Having the collection accessible from one location — or, as today with digital libraries, equally accessible from numerous locations — is an essential component of the universal library that no ancient library except Alexandria accomplished.

Gabriel Naudé's Advice on Establishing a Library

We have to wait until the Renaissance before notions of a universal library reappear in Western civilization. As a phrase, "universal library" can be traced back at least to the Swiss scholar Conrad Gessner's 1545 compendium *Bibliotheca Universalis*. But by *bibliotheca*, Gessner did not mean a library as we mean it today. The *Bibliotheca Universalis* did for the known Greek, Latin, and Hebrew literature of the sixteenth century what Callimachus' "Tables" had done for ancient Greek literature. Hans Fischer in "Conrad Gessner as Bibliographer and Encyclopedist" describes the work.

> Gessner's *Bibliotheca universalis* was to comprise three parts. The first of these was a list of authors from every period arranged in alphabetical order. This was to be followed by a systematic exposition of all areas of knowledge as treated in literature and would include individual comprehensive treatises. Finally, he planned a dictionary of arts and sciences. . . . [It] offered the academic world a 1,264 folio-page index of authors, complete with biographical details. (271)

Because of this great work and its later editions, Gessner is often called the father of bibliography. As with bibliographies today, the first step to either collection or scholarship is to identify what works exist on a subject, and comprehensive bibliographies of the sort Gessner compiled are necessary steps toward a universal library.

They are also necessary because of the scope of what such a library could possibly contain by the seventeenth century was prodigious. At least since Alvin Toffler warned us of "information overload" in the nineteen seventies, the received wisdom is that we are living through an unprecedented information explosion. While it is undoubtedly true that the amount of information is increasing at unprecedented rates, the *perception* that we already have more information than we can successfully process has been around since at least the sixteenth century. Gessner himself complained of the "confusing and harmful abundance of books" in his preface to the *Bibliotheca universalis* (quoted in Blair 11). By the late seventeenth century, the philosopher and sometime librarian Gottfried Leibniz complained of the "'horrible mass of books which keeps on growing,' so that eventually, he feared, 'the disorder will become nearly insurmountable'" (Yeo "Solution" 62). In the eighteenth century, Diderot prophesied that "as centuries pass by, the mass of works grows endlessly, and one can foresee a time when it will be almost as difficult to educate oneself in a library, as in the universe, and almost as fast to seek a truth subsisting in nature, as lost among an immense number of books" (Diderot "Encyclopedia"). The Ptolomies' main problem was finding and copying the books for their library at Alexandria. In the centuries after the invention of the printing press, the problem was figuring out what to select for a universal library and how to make the works in the library accessible. Hence the development of reference works, miscellanies, and such works as Louis Ellies Du Pin's early eighteenth century *Bibliothèque universelle des historiens*, translated in 1709 with the catchy title, *The Universal Library of Historians; (viz.) the Oriental, Greek, Latin, French, German, Spanish, Italian, English, and others: containing an account of their lives; the abridgment, chronology and geography of their histories; with critical observations on their style and character; and a catalogue of the several editions of their works*.

For a fuller development of the concept of a universal library in the seventeenth century, we should turn to Gabriel Naudé's *Advice on Establishing a Library* (1st ed., 1627, 2nd ed., 1644; translated into English, 1661). Naudé's treatise is one of the earliest works on librarianship in any modern sense, and lays out a plan for systematically collecting a research library. Though he had developed a number of libraries, when he wrote *Advice* Naudé was the librarian at the De Memses library in Paris. After years of travel, he was summoned back to Paris in 1642 to develop Cardinal Richelieu's library. Richelieu promptly died, but the plan for the library was saved by his successor, Cardinal Mazarin. Naudé developed Cardinal Mazarin's personal library, the Bibliotheque Mazarine, and requested it be open to the public, thus creating the first public library in France. At that time, "only three libraries let scholars request any book: The Bodleian at Oxford, the Bibliotheca Ambrosiana in Milan, and the Angelica library in Rome" (Clarke 333).

Opening libraries to the public, especially large libraries, marks the second step in the ultimate universal library: a library with a comprehensive collection that is also accessible by the people rather than just the rulers. Until relatively recently in human history, most libraries were private, the property of royals or the rich, and served to collect but not disseminate knowledge. The same is true of archives. In "The Ordinariness of the Archive," Thomas Osborne writes that "before the invention of the modern notion of the public, archives nearly always take this sovereign, non-public form," and that even in the modern period, "the first archives were centralized expressions of enlightened despotism: Peter the Great at St Petersburg in 1720 and Maria Theresa at Vienna in 1749. In France the revolutionaries in 1790 ordered the creation of the National Archives; but the key date for the emergence of the really modern kind of archival spirit is surely 25 July 1794, the date of a decree opening up those archives to the public" (55). This modern change in the archival spirit applies to all libraries. Naudé was among the first to develop the idea of a comprehensive, "universal library" open to the public and collecting works on almost every subject, libraries the historian Jonathan Israel, in *Radical Enlightenment*, has called "workshops of the early Enlightenment." "It was assuredly in Europe's libraries," Israel writes, "that the opening up of fresh horizons and many revolutionary new insights of the period originated" (119), a claim analogous to Benjamin Franklin's belief that the social libraries prevalent in the American colonies helped give Americans a political education.

One establishes a library, according to Naudé, to preserve the minds of distinguished persons who have transmitted through writing "what was most noble about themselves" (5). For the person establishing it, the establishment also brings fame and glory, as well as a personal benefit of having a large research library at one's disposal: it makes one cosmopolitan, since with such a library one "may know all, see all, and be ignorant of nothing" (9). One might even be enlightened by so much knowledge. A collection for a private person can be partial, but a collection for the public should be general and contain all the major books on every subject; ideally, all library users should find what they seek, and no book is so bad that someone, sometime may want to consult it. In a wonderful metaphor, Naudé compares libraries to "the meadow of Seneca, where every living creature finds that which is most proper for it" (18). They should also be arranged by subject so people can find the books they need, since no collection of disorganized books can really be called a library.

The universal library could not even then contain every book, and so selection is inevitable. Naudé justified including reference books and anthologies because "the brevity of our life and the multitude of things which we are now obliged to know if we are to be reckoned among the learned do not permit us to do all by ourselves" (31). Nevertheless, even if true universality could not be achieved, the library can achieve what we might call representative universality. A library should have the best authors and the best editions, including not only common but rare works, both in their original languages and in translations into the common language of the library users (which in Naudé's case was Latin and French), and the best books on every subject. For Naudé there were clearly no books off limits, no *Index Librorum Prohibitorum*. This policy contrasted with the collection policies of most post-Reformation libraries, in both Catholic and Protestant countries (see Israel 118). The devout with no desire to be enlightened or cosmopolitan could comfortably consume devotional literature of their own confession and any non-threatening works, the way political blog readers of today, for example, tend to consume only writing that already confirms their prejudices. Such partial libraries were the "Daily Me" of the seventeenth century.

The logic — what one might call the logic of counter-Enlightenment — is similar, whether one is a twenty-first century political ideologue or a seventeenth century Catholic. It is the logic at work in the legend that the caliph Omar ordered the destruction of the Library of Alexandria in 641 AD. According to one account, Omar's order for the destruction of the books was irrefutable from the standpoint of the fanatic: "if their content is in accordance with the book of Allah, we may do without them, for in that case the book of Allah more than suffices. If, on the other hand, they contain matter not in accordance with the book of Allah, there can be no need to preserve them" (quoted in Canfora 98). It is the logic of every censor, every fanatic, every ideologue.

Such logic is foreign to research libraries today, both the great national and university libraries around the world. What should surprise us with Naudé is the absence of this parochial dogmatism. He wanted libraries to be both universal and public, so that everyone could be exposed not just to comforting dogma, but even to heresy. Partly, the purpose is enlightenment and understanding.

> I affirm that all these authors are requisite to a library . . . since it is certain that the knowledge of these books is so useful and valuable to him who can consider and draw profit from all that he sees that it provides him a thousand openings and new conceptions, which, being received by a mind that is open, inquiring, and free from prejudice . . . make him speak to the purpose on all subjects, deliver him from the admiration which is the true mark of our weakness, and enable him to discourse upon whatsoever presents itself with a great deal more judg-

ment, foresight, and resolution than many persons of letters and merit are used to do. (23-24).

Libraries should even collect erroneous and dangerous books, because these provide a contrast with better books, "like thorns among the roses," and allow people see them in order to test their wits against them. This seems to me a more justifiable reason to collect bad books than the hope that in reading them the public would eventually get a "taste" for great literature. In order to refute heretical books, scholars must be able to read them, and even "God permits us to profit from our enemies" (27-28). Such reasoning works even for the devout, as long as they believe in reason and are not fanatics. The same reasoning now stands behind most academic and public libraries. The defense is not that controversial books are right, or even good, but that they are part of the world, and educated, enlightened, unprejudiced minds should read to learn and test their beliefs rather than just to confirm their prejudices. A daring idea for his time and for ours.

The pattern is the same, and is much like the cloistered, stultifying mindset that Naudé was battling in the early seventeenth century and that enlightened libraries actively resist. Open inquiry and intellectual freedom are cornerstones of Enlightenment thought and foundational values for most libraries academic and public. The reason libraries collect books on all subjects is not because they are neutral and just want to represent all points of view. Academic libraries, for example, do not build extensive collections of the sort Naudé envisioned because of their neutrality, or because they think every idea should have equal representation and be considered equally useful or valid. They build those collections to support the habit of open inquiry and the increase of knowledge. If librarians buy books promoting totalitarianism, it is not because they think totalitarianism is right or true. To the extent that public libraries serve as the "people's university," their collections serve the same purpose, to allow at least the possibility of open inquiry even if few take advantage of it. Examining our country and culture reveals plenty of people hostile to open inquiry, intellectual freedom, and reading to learn rather than reinforce their prejudices. When those people write books, we collect them so that open minds can be informed *about* them, not *by* them, and can test our beliefs against the arguments of those who wish to shut down argument. Naudé understood this in the early seventeenth century.

Diderot and the Encyclopédie

The Enlightenment era saw a dramatic increase in the production of encyclopedias. The information overload that we often hear about today was *felt* as early as the seventeenth century, as we saw with Gessner's response to the number of books available at the time. Writers and compilers of dictionaries and encyclopedias responded to this problem just as Naudé and other librarians had to. As Richard Yeo tells us in *Encyclopedic Visions*, "the authors of these early dictionaries were very much aware of the problem of ordering and communicating knowledge, and these works can be seen as responses to what contemporaries perceived as a knowledge explosion, witnessed in the rapid multiplication of books and the pace of discovery in geographical exploration and in the physical sciences" (xiii). The most important encyclopedia project during the Enlightenment was undoubtedly the *En-

cyclopédie project. "The *Encyclopédie*, edited by Denis Diderot (1713-84) and Jean Le Rond d'Alembert (1717-83) from 1751, and completed in seventeen volumes of text and eleven volumes of plates in 1772, became almost synonymous with Enlightenment" (xii).

The basic facts of the *Encyclopédie* can be briefly stated, although Philipp Blom provides a delightful history of the project in his *Enlightening the World*. In 1745, bookseller André-François Le Breton contracted with Godefroy Sellius and John Mills to translate Ephraim Chambers' *Cyclopaedia*. First published in 1728, the *Cyclopaedia* became one of the most popular scientific dictionaries of the eighteenth century. It combined alphabetical entries with a respect for the integrity and interrelation of different branches of knowledge, which "gave his work a reputation during the eighteenth century that established a benchmark for all encyclopaedias" (Yeo *Encyclopedic* 123). The full title of the work gives some indication of Chambers' ambitions:

> Cyclopaedia, or, An Universal Dictionary of Arts and Sciences: Containing the Definitions of the Terms, and Accounts of the Things Signify'd Thereby, in the Several Arts, both Liberal and Mechanical, and the Several Sciences, Human and Divine: the Figures, Kinds, Properties, Productions, Preparations, and Uses, of Things Natural and Artificial; the Rise, Progress, and State of Things Ecclesiastical, Civil, Military, and Commercial: with the Several Systems, Sects, Opinions, etc; among Philosophers, Divines, Mathematicians, Physicians, Antiquaries, Criticks, etc.: The Whole Intended as a Course of Ancient and Modern Learning.

A second edition appeared in 1738, and by the seventeen forties was a natural standard upon which to base a French translation. Le Breton announced the plan and invited subscriptions in April 1745 for an *Encyclopédie, or Dictionnaire universel de arts & des sciences*. However, Mills' French was inadequate; he translated very little of the work and what he did translate needed correction. Le Breton retrenched, and by late 1745 had hired a new editor, the mathematician Abbé Jean-Paul Gua de Malves. Gua de Malves lasted but thirteen months, after which Jean d'Alembert and Denis Diderot became the editors for what was still to be a translation of Chambers' *Cyclopedia*. (Blom 35-40).

Instead, the *Encyclopédie* became something much larger, in both size and importance, than Chambers' two-volume scientific dictionary. It was both a reference work and a manifesto. Robert Darnton argues in *The Business of Enlightenment: a Publishing History of the Encyclopédie, 1775-1800* that to "ask whether the *Encyclopédie* was a reference work or a manifesto of Enlightenment is to pose a false problem, for it was meant to combine those characteristics, and it was presented as a combination of them, by its promoters as well as its authors" (523), and furthermore, that the "contemporary understanding of the book should be taken seriously because it shows the extent to which the *Encyclopédie* was identified with the Enlightenment in the eighteenth century" (524). Never before had a reference book become emblematic of a movement. The *Encyclopédie* embodied the Enlightenment as the *Communist Manifesto* embodies communism. Darnton further argues that the *Encyclopédie* did indeed present something of an "ism." "It showed that knowledge was ordered, not random; that the ordering principle was reason working on sense data, not revelation speaking through tradition; and that rational standards, when applied to contemporary institutions, would expose absurdity and iniquity everywhere" (539-40). In his history, Darnton shows that in the *Encyclopédie* the ideals of a political order based on principles of liberty and equality were "expressed in print, disseminated in the social order, embodied in institutions, and incorporated in a new vision of the world" (545).

In the *Encyclopédie* article on "*Encyclopédie*," which Philipp Blom considers "perhaps the most important in all the twenty-eight volumes of the work" (151), Diderot states the project's purpose:

> the purpose of an encyclopedia is to collect knowledge disseminated around the globe; to set forth its general system to the men with whom we live, and transmit it to those who will come after us, so that the work of preceding centuries will not become useless to the centuries to come; and so that our offspring, becoming better instructed, will at the same time become more virtuous and happy, and that we should not die without having rendered a service to the human race.

And indeed, the *Encyclopédie* does attempt to give an impression of the world of knowledge at that moment. There are articles on Asparagus and Atomism, Farts and Freemasons, Sovereignty and Sugar. Diderot wanted all knowledge on every subject available to everyone, and the most practical way to accomplish this goal of the Enlightenment was a universal encyclopedia. The *Encyclopédie* is especially notable in our context for two things — its attention to the mundane rather than just the great, and its relative placement of theology in the structure of knowledge.

While d'Alembert would not include biographies of "great men," the *Encyclopédie* does include numerous articles on trades and crafts of the time. Richard Yeo places the *Encyclopédie* in a larger context of libraries and the organization of knowledge. Following Karl Popper, he argues that libraries and encyclopedias are part of a "third world" of knowledge that could be used to recreate the knowledge of sense or cognition (so perhaps Frederick Crunden was not so far off after all.) "Imagine, [Popper] said, a scenario in which 'all our machines and tools are destroyed, and all our subjective learning, including the knowledge of machines and tools, and how to use them. But *libraries and our capacity to learn from them* survive. Clearly, after much suffering, our world may get going again'" (2). Though Popper is clearly discussing libraries, Yeo's association of libraries with encyclopedias is relevant for our discussion, for both the encyclopedia and the universal library are ways to organize and disseminate all the important knowledge in the world. In *Encyclopedic Visions*, Yeo writes that Diderot considered the *Encyclopédie* a "time capsule of the Enlightenment. In the event of a catastrophe, it would be a summary of intellectual accomplishments to be reactivated by a later age," and that the encyclopedia as time capsule "is the most powerful encyclopaedic vision: a work containing the collective knowledge of a community which might be put together again if all the other books were lost" (3). In fact, something like this happened, at least on a small scale. According to Blom, "accuracy was a point of pride in all the illustrations" and that "some of them are so precise in their descriptions that they have been used to reconstruct entire manufacturing processes." In 1796, the "College of Military Engineering in Constantinople accepted the necessity for reform in order to construct better artillery . . . [and]

found everything they needed to know about canon manufacture in a copy of the *Encyclopédie* that had made its way to the Ottoman capital" (263).

The *Encyclopédie* was also noteworthy for considering theology a subset of philosophy, thus engendering acrimonious and lasting critiques from French Catholic authorities. Orthodox Christian thought at the time, which comprised most official and public thought in Europe, considered theology and revelation to be superior to human reason and philosophy. That is still the case, but orthodox Christians seldom control modern states. The orthodox had not progressed beyond the view of medieval scholastics that philosophy was the handmaiden of theology. In the *Système Figuré des Connoissances Humaines* ("Map of the System of Human Knowledge") included in the *Encyclopédie*, knowledge is divided into Memory, Reason, and Imagination. Reason itself is divided into the Science of Nature, the Science of Man, and (placed slightly lower than the others) the Science of God, and in the structure of the chart, Religion seems equivalent to Superstition, Divinity, and Black Magic — which is more or less what Diderot believed to be true. In line with Enlightenment philosophy, human reason provided us with the tools to understand the world, and religion was but one part of human study, and lower down the scale of human knowledge than ethics or arithmetic. The *Encyclopédie* treated all subjects as a modern university does — as equally important objects of study, none grander than another because of supposedly divine origins.

Besides its equal consideration of all knowledge and its concomitant devaluing of religion, the *Encyclopédie* also promoted Enlightenment in its politics. The Encyclopedists wrote under a regime of official censorship. Though by the end of the project, the censors and authorities let the project continue unofficially, every article had the potential to send the editor or authors to prison. Diderot, who had once been imprisoned for a month for writing works considered scandalous, was quite aware of this, and had effected his release from prison by promising the Chief of Police to submit all his works to censorship or accept life imprisonment (Blom 59). Nevertheless, the *Encyclopédie* cries out for reason and liberty and against superstition and privilege in both direct and indirect fashion.

For a good example of the direct appeal, consider Diderot's opening in his article on "Political Authority":

> No man has received from nature the right to command others. Liberty is a gift from heaven, and each individual of the same species has the right to enjoy it as soon as he enjoys the use of reason. If nature has established any authority, it is paternal control; but paternal control has its limits, and in the state of nature it would terminate when the children could take care of themselves. Any other authority comes from another origin than nature. If one seriously considers this matter, one will always go back to one of these two sources: either the force and violence of an individual who has seized it, or the consent of those who have submitted to it by a contract made or assumed between them and the individual on whom they have bestowed authority. (Diderot, "Political")

No cry for liberty and equality could be more direct than this, and in one paragraph Diderot summarizes key themes of Enlightenment republicanism: individual liberty, equality before the law, sovereignty from the consent of the governed. Any political power or privileges possessed by priests or aristocrats or monarchs are unnatural and the result of violence, not mandated by God.

Often enough, however, political or anti-religious sentiment was less direct. Blom discusses many of the strategies the Encyclopedists used, such as "hiding progressive opinion behind established authorities," or smuggling minor political critiques into articles on non-political topics (146). The articles on economics could be more progressive than those on politics, since they did not explicitly criticize the power of Church or Crown. Thus, there are economically liberal articles on free markets by Turgot and criticisms of the lack of innovation and competition of guilds by Faiguet. Sometimes the implicit critique was buried in subject headings. For example, "readers wanting to inform themselves about dukes first found under the headword *DUC* 'a great bird that feeds only at night and has on its head feathers in the forms of ears,' and only then did the article deal with a member of the high nobility" (Blom 154). *ROI* ("King") received similar treatment. Cross-references also played their part in the criticism. The entry on Cannibals has a cross-reference to *Eucharist*, Freedom of Thought to *Intolerance & Jesus Christ*, and "Office (reminding everyone of the positions bought by incompetent courtiers for tax exemptions, pensions, and bribes) was accompanied by '*See: Morals, Morality, and Ethics*'" (154).

In the *Encyclopédie*, we see a microcosm of the universal library of the Enlightenment. Both encyclopedias and libraries are concerned with the collection, organization, and dissemination of information, and the ideal library might be contained in the ideal encyclopedia. Both a true universal library accessible to all and a truly comprehensive encyclopedia exemplify the scientific and political principles of the Enlightenment in the domain of information. As we have seen, Enlightenment thinking stipulates that every subject is worthy of investigation, and that the results of that investigation should be published and made available to everyone for study and criticism in an atmosphere of reason and freedom. A universal library or an encyclopedia (literally, a "circle of knowledge") are examples of how the results of investigation are made public. For my purposes, it is significant that the book (or set of books) that became most identified with the Enlightenment was not simply a political manifesto, but a work of reference intended to spread useful knowledge, liberty, and equality as broadly as possible.

H.G. Wells and the World Brain

Let us skip forward two centuries, from an age when books were still scarce and expensive to an age where people felt buried by books and information, the age we still inhabit. Perhaps the oddest project related to a universal library is H.G. Wells' proposed "World Brain" (1938). The World Brain (or World Encyclopaedia, or New Encyclopaedism, or World Knowledge Apparatus — Wells was fond of portentous initial capitalized letters) would gather together the knowledge scattered about the world in the minds of experts and channel it towards the world's leaders. The universal library, as we have seen, must contain the world's knowledge, or at least a significant representative amount of the world's knowledge. However, that knowledge must be accessible to be useful. A disorganized collection is as useless as no collection at all. By the early twentieth century, when Wells was working out his idea of the World Brain, the number and rate of published books was overwhelming, quite literally in the case of large research libraries that began a long period of expansion in the middle of the century. Even by 1934, the philosopher José Ortega y Gasset complained not only that there were so many books no scholar could read them all, but that they were "being produced every day in torrential abundance" (153); indeed, Ortega argued that there were so many books that instead of trying to collect them all, the "mission of the librarian" was to filter out the bad books so scholars would not have to waste their time with them. Wells tried to develop a way to overcome information overload.

For Wells, the World Problem was that the scale of human life and the production of knowledge had increased dramatically in the previous few decades, but our ability to process and use that knowledge had changed little in two hundred years. There was a "wide gap between . . . the at present unassembled and unexploited best thought and knowledge in the world, and the ideas and acts not simply of the masses of common people, but of those who direct public affairs. . . . We live in a world of unused and misapplied knowledge and skill" (6). Wells believed that the world had so many wars and world problems because people did not know enough; they were unenlightened. While a generation later Adorno and Horkheimer thought the enlightened earth radiated calamity, Wells at least knew that most of the earth had never benefitted from an age of enlightenment. Most of the world's people had remained unaffected by the Enlightenment project, with its emphasis on science and useful knowledge and its democratic republican politics. Wells believed that if spread widely enough, science could "enlighten and animate our politics and rule the world" (11). Furthermore, if the world did not somehow learn to use knowledge adequately, then dire consequences would result. With the increase in knowledge came a "monstrous increase of destructive power," and Wells opined that without a World Brain, we would "knock ourselves to pieces" (29), as indeed happened very soon after that, though more science probably would not have stopped Hitler from invading Poland.

Like many utopian thinkers, Wells had a plan to solve this problem that would require only the organized effort of every university, research institute, and government in the world. A "*World Encyclopedia* . . . is the means whereby we can solve the problem of that jig-saw puzzle and bring all the scattered and ineffective mental wealth of our world into something like a common understanding, and into effective reaction upon our vulgar everyday political, social and economic life" (11). While the World Brain was a metaphor, the World Encyclopedia was not. Wells envisioned an actual encyclopedia of thirty or forty volumes, consisting of "selections, extracts, quotations, very carefully assembled with the approval of outstanding authorities in each subject, carefully collated and edited and critically presented" (14), kept in every school and library in the world so that it could be easily consulted by anyone (49). It would contain the best available knowledge in every field of inquiry, and become a "mental clearing house for the mind, a depot where knowledge and ideas are received, sorted, summarized, digested, clarified and compared." The World Encyclopedia would be constantly updated as well, and for that purpose the organizers "would be in continual correspondence with every university, every research institution, every competent discussion, every survey, every statistical bureau in the world" (49), and all this in the days before email.

It would make knowledge widely available, possibly even on microfilm, a new technology at the time that excited Wells a great deal. He predicted we might have "microscopic libraries of record, in which a photograph of every important book and document in the world will be stowed away and made easily available for the inspection of the student.... The time is close at hand when any student, in any part of the world, will be able to sit with his projector in his own study at his or her convenience to examine *any* book, *any* document, in an exact replica" (54). Indeed, in the nineteen thirties the technology was just emerging to create such a possibility, and, as we shall see in the next section on the Memex, by the forties Vannevar Bush was thinking about a machine to do just that. Such a dream may never be realized, though for legal and not technological reasons. Lengthy copyright laws forbid it. One irony of Wells' statement is that his own book, published in 1938, is still under copyright, and cannot legally be viewed by everyone in the world even in replica. In the United States, most books published after 1923 are subject to copyright. Another irony is that Wells believed the World Encyclopedia should consist mostly of extracts, rather than new writing, which copyright would also prevent (although the World Encyclopedia might be considered "fair use").

But back to the World Encyclopedia. More than a clearing house, it would become the standard of truth for the entire world. "Its contents would be the standard source of material for the instructional side of school and college work, for the verification of facts and the testing of statements — everywhere in the world" (14). Wells had faith — and *faith* is the best word for it — that just about every question in the world could be settled by science, and that the encyclopedia would settle those questions by providing the most accurate and up-to-date scientific answer available. "Such an Encyclopaedia would play the role of an undogmatic Bible to a world culture.... It would hold the world together mentally" (14). To the objection that such an encyclopedia, an undogmatic Bible that served as the standard of truth was impossible because of conflicts within knowledge itself, Wells countered that such conflicts were quite small, and confined to the margins of knowledge. To get an idea of how broad Wells' definition of *science* could be, his comment should be quoted at length.

> You have all heard and you have all probably been irritated or bored by the assertion that no two people think alike, . . . that science is always contradicting itself, that theologians and economists can never agree. . . . But I am inclined to think that most people overrate the apparent differences in the world of opinion today. . . . Even in theology a psychological analysis reduces many flat contradictions to differences in terminology. (15)

Even in theology! It should be clear from this that Wells was not speaking of *science* in the rather narrow sense we often use, of natural science, or even social science. *Science* is the organized knowledge about every possible subject, all reducible to positivistic interpretation. In this regard, Wells belongs undoubtedly to one strain of the Enlightenment, the strain represented by Godwin perhaps, or Bentham, the strain that acclaims the benefits of the scientific method without the equally Enlightenment skepticism about its scope.

In another reply to the same criticism, it becomes clearer that Wells has inherited both the philosophical and political Enlightenment.

> [Critics] will say that an Encyclopaedia must always be tendentious and within certain limits — but they are very wide

limits — that must be true. A World Encyclopaedia will have by its very nature to be what is called *liberal*. An Encyclopaedia appealing to all mankind can admit no narrowing dogmas without at the same time admitting corrective criticism. It will have to be guarded editorially and with the utmost jealous against the incessant invasion of narrowing propaganda. It will have a general flavor of what many people will call skepticism. Myth, however venerated, it must treat as myth and not as a symbolical rendering of some higher truth or any such evasion. Visions and projects and theories it must distinguish from bedrock fact.... (55)

There are many possible criticisms one might make of this statement, and from various perspectives. Some would perhaps criticize Wells' Eurocentrism as well as his faith in science and liberalism. However, Wells' skeptical, scientific view of religious dogma is typical of Western intellectuals, and hardly surprising. His view of the world and the World Encyclopedia are not that much different from Diderot's.

A stronger criticism might be that the skepticism he makes so much of does not go far enough. Wells is skeptical of myths parading as facts, but not skeptical enough of the reach of science and its methods. In this, he might be the victim of a common problem: that Enlightenment science progressed more rapidly than Enlightenment politics. Splitting the atom is easier than achieving world peace, because the method that works so well in the first works hardly at all in the second. As W. Boyd Rayward, a stern critic of Wells' World Brain, put it, Wells "clearly saw himself as a member of a newly emergent technocratic elite in whom 'Science' had vested access to the simplification and absoluteness of Truth amidst all the clamor, strife, ambiguity and confusion of the modern age. . . . He seems committed to the idea that political and social decisions are reducible to questions of scientific — and economic — fact" (569). This conflation of politics and science and the view that political problems are simply scientific problems waiting to be solved through instrumental rationality resembles the strain of Enlightenment thought Adorno and Horkheimer criticized as well, but Wells' liberalism is a far cry from the totalitarianism of a Hitler or a Stalin. His instrumental rationality is in the service of liberalism, whatever his flaws.

Mostly by reading *World Brain* in the context of selected novels Wells also wrote — especially *A Modern Utopia* (1905) and *The Shape of Things to Come* (1934) — Rayward tries to make the case that the World Encyclopedia notion is totalitarian in nature, that ideally it would become a standard of truth by force, and those who disagreed with the facts would be eliminated if they inconveniently dissented. Some of Wells' fiction, especially the earlier *Modern Utopia*, does indeed allow for this possibility, but one has to read *World Brain* against the grain to get such a reading, and to ignore Wells' own conception of the World Encyclopedia as something that does not immediately challenge the entrenched tyrants and dictators of the world. "It is not the sort of thing to which they would be directly antagonistic. It is not ostensibly anti-*them*. It would have a terrible and ultimately destructive aloofness. They would not easily realize its significance for all that they do and are" (23). Like the *Encyclopédie*, the World Encyclopedia could oppose tyranny indirectly through its very existence. In *World Brain*, Wells lamented the rise of tyranny and dictatorships, "the threats of nationalist aggression and the suppression of free discussion in many parts of the world," and the fact that "vehement *state-ism* [dominated] affairs over large regions of the civilized world," and that "everywhere liberty [was] threatened or outraged" (35). Whatever scientistic tendencies might emerge in his fiction, these are not the words of a totalitarian. The World Encyclopedia would persuade by its truth, not by force, at least as Wells presents his views in *World Brain*.

Rayward rightly asks what might happen if the World Brain were to malfunction, but this possibility is less terrifying absent the totalitarian world order Wells supposedly favored. Though I believe the political critique goes too far, Rayward is on stronger ground with his epistemological critique and gets at the heart of why Wells' vision must ultimately fail. According to Rayward, the "store of human knowledge is almost incalculably massive in scale, is largely viewpoint dependent, is fragmented, complex, ceaselessly in dispute and always under revision" (572), and because of this a World Encyclopedia as a standard of truth, an undogmatic Bible for the world, could never exist as a sure guide to action. We do not need Wells' faith in boundless science to be somewhat skeptical of Rayward's extreme epistemological relativism, though. The store of human knowledge may indeed be incalculably massive in scale, which might preclude it being gathered into forty convenient volumes and distributed to one's local library. Wells even accounted for the fact that such knowledge is complex and always being revised — as would be the World Encyclopedia.

However, that such knowledge is viewpoint-dependent Wells would consider quite irrelevant, and we can, too, without turning into totalitarians. Philosophers often define knowledge as justified true belief, and while this definition itself has problems, much of human knowledge is not, in fact, viewpoint-dependent. Opinion is viewpoint-dependent, and the problem is more often the lack of a common standard of reason or truth, rather than fragmented and subjective knowledge. As an example, consider the aggressive arguments between creationists and scientists over evolution. Creationists base their claims on evidence that has no independent verification — the book of Genesis. Scientists base their arguments on evidence and public reasons that everyone can see. To claim that we cannot have scientific knowledge about evolution, even if it is incomplete, because creationists dispute the evidence is ludicrous. We might as well claim that we cannot know for sure if Zeus sends thunderbolts from heaven, because the ancient Greeks certainly thought he did. Political disagreements often result from a clash of moral or religious beliefs rather than a clash of viewpoint-dependent knowledge. That Andrew Carnegie and the Catholic Church differed on the benefits of alms-giving has nothing to do with conflicts in knowledge as such.

Wells' ultimate problem is not that all knowledge is "viewpoint dependent," but that he neglects the scope of science, of what can actually be proven indisputably with public evidence. The earth revolves around the sun. Splitting atoms can create explosions. These we can know with certainty. But outside the natural sciences, such knowledge becomes shakier. The social sciences have yet to produce a body of knowledge that explains and predicts human behavior in the way that natural scientists can explain and predict natural phenomena. If Nobel Prize winning economists disagree radically on whether a country is in a recession or how a recession might be ended, that is a sign that social science has no such rigorous body of knowledge. We can know *some* things about human behavior, general rules that perhaps usually apply. Historically, for example, we know that generally the rule of law, democratic government, and free markets tend to produce more wealth than their opposites, and that if those markets are unregulated the wealth will gravitate to the top few percent of the population. Another problem is that the standards of truth Wells accepted — enlightenment standards of truth and reason — are not always persuasive, not because they can be refuted, but because they can be ignored, and will be ignored if they conflict with compelling or psychologically necessary fictions. For critics of Enlightenment such as Alasdair MacIntyre, this fact undermines the claims of Enlightenment completely. Obviously I disagree, but it is seems clear that what people believe is often motivated by myth, comfort, convenience, or psychological necessity rather than the quest for reason and truth, even where it can be attained. The range of genuinely disputed knowledge in the world combined with psychological or religious disagreements means that Wells could not have been right that *science* could answer all our questions about politics or religion, and that even if it *could* there would still be dissent. Nevertheless, the fact that more and better knowledge cannot create a perfect world does not mean that it cannot create a better one.

Vannevar Bush and the Memex

While the world was busy knocking its brains out during World War II, Vannevar Bush directed the Office of Scientific Research and Development, a group charged with organizing scientific research for the United States government. While an engineering professor at MIT during the nineteen thirties, he had invented a code-breaking machine that was later used to break Japanese codes in World War II. He had also co-invented a machine dubbed the "rapid selector," which with the proper programming could select multiple bits of microfilm from a few hundred thousand images based on selected criteria. But Bush's most memorable invention was one that never came to fruition, at least in the form he envisioned it: the Memex.

In the July 1945 issue of *The Atlantic*, Bush published an essay that provided an early vision of what today's computer and Internet can achieve. He was worried about the "growing mountain of research" and the danger that researchers were "being bogged down today as specialization extends," just as researchers had been since the seventeenth century. "The investigator," he writes, "is staggered by the findings and conclusions of thousands of other workers — conclusions which he cannot find time to grasp, much less to remember, as they appear. Yet specialization becomes increasingly necessary for progress, and the effort to bridge between disciplines is correspondingly superficial" (Bush 88). This statement reformulates Wells' concerns, but from the point of scientific researchers rather than world leaders. Our individual minds cannot keep up with the production of our collective mind. Much like Wells — or for that matter Gessner, Naudé, Diderot, or Ortega before him — Bush noted that "our methods of transmitting and reviewing the results of research are generations old and by now are totally inadequate for their purpose" and that "that publication has been extended far beyond our present ability to make real use of the record" (89).

Bush believed that the technology was theoretically available to solve this problem, though unlike Wells he envisioned a machine to solve the problem for the individual researcher rather than a reference book to solve it for the entire world. Instead of a World Brain, we get what by 1945 standards would have been the ultimate help for the individual brain — the Memex. The Memex is a combination desk and computer-like apparatus. On top of the desk are "slanting translucent screens," one for projecting microfilm images and the other for taking notes, using the attached keyboard or a stylus device on the second screen (102). The files themselves would be microfilm, presumably available for purchase and ready to be inserted into the machine, and there would be plenty of room for such microfilm, since "if the user inserted 5000 pages of material a day it would take him hundreds of years to fill the repository, so he can be profligate and enter material freely" (103). One can only wonder what Bush would have thought about the availability of computer memory today.

The Memex would become a universal library for the individual researcher, though Bush's assumption seems to be that microfilm reels would be readily available for anyone needing them. The researcher could call up any book or article or photograph, scroll through numerous documents, and make notes linking the documents together. The problem of traditional systems of organization is the indexing. In a paper world, a piece of information could be in only one place, organized in some schematic, but impersonal way, as in a library. Bush argued that the human mind works by association, and wrote of researchers (and in central libraries, librarians) creating "trails" of association through the forest of microfilmed documents analogous to our hyperlinks. In "Memex II," he speculates that these trails could improve the progress of knowledge. "The race progresses as the experience and reasoning of one generation is handed on to the next. Can a son inherit the memex of his father, or the disciple that of his master, refined and polished over the years, and go on from there?" (183). If we increase knowledge by standing on the shoulders of giants, how much better it would be for us if the giants had left their thought trails on a Memex.

Much like in Wells' utopia, in Bush's vision all the world's information has been reduced to microfilm available at a reasonable price to everyone, as many people mistakenly believe today that most information is digitized and readily available to anyone with an Internet connection. In a later 1959 essay, "Memex II," he goes on about the ease of actually acquiring material for research: "Professional societies will no longer print papers. Instead they will send him lists of titles with brief abstracts. And he can then order individual papers of sets to come on tape, complete, of course, with photographs and diagrams" (172). Still later, in "Memex Revisited" (1965), he exhibited the practical thinking of the scientist in terms of materials, but not other costs. He noted that the "material for a microfilm private library might cost a nickel, and it could be mailed anywhere for a few cents. . . . The entire material of a private library in reduced film form would go on ten eight-and-one-half-by-eleven-inch sheets. Once that was available, with the reproduction methods now available, duplicates in large quantities could probably be turned out for a few cents apiece beyond the cost of materials" (208). As with the current debate about ebooks, Bush implies that the cost of information lay primarily in its medium, ignoring the costs of the information production itself. Microfilm is cheaper than print, so information will be cheaper, as people resist paying as much for ebooks today as they do for print books. If the cost of information were correlated with the cost of the medium of distribution, then digital books and articles would be nearly free, which of course they are not.

To some extent, his future is our present, as long as the researcher has the resources of large academic libraries to draw upon. However, he never envisioned the digitization of information, nor the shifting economics of information that would escalate costs well beyond the reach of most individuals. Wells thought in world historical terms, but Bush thought always in terms of the scholar or researcher within a bureaucracy. Regarding information storage, hyperlinking, and the personal nature of interaction with information, his Memex presaged the Internet and the personal computer, but the amount of information he believed might be available has been limited by economic and legal arrangements he never considered. Professional societies still exist, for example, and many still publish articles, but instead of printing papers, these articles are often published by commercial science publishers, and the contents of their journals are prohibitively expensive for many libraries, not to mention individual scholars. Bush reasoned as though legal and financial restrictions on the availability of knowledge did not exist, even for scholars. In his universal library, information just appeared, cheaply and abundantly, to whomever might want to use it.

Google

The dream of a universal library is ancient, and the dream of a universal library organized and accessible to all has existed since at least the seventeenth century. Despite the rapid increase in published information of all kinds, the dream is still as vibrant as ever, though the way to achieve the dream has changed. Where the Ptolomies copied by force every scroll they could find, and Naudé gave advice on how to organize a universal library by subject, and we have long had a network of American research libraries supporting scholars, today we have Google, whose "mission is to organize the world's information and make it universally accessible and useful" (Google). Google does no such thing, of course, and at its best finds bits of the world's information with search algorithms, but its self-declared mission is a contemporary iteration of Naudé's goal, or of Diderot's. The most popular encyclopedia in the world, Wikipedia, also reaches for the Enlightenment goal of making useful information accessible. Between the two of them, Google and Wikipedia have for many people created the illusion of a universal library. While working on this book, I discussed the "universal library" chapter with numerous people, mostly professors or librarians. When I would describe Naudé's library, or Wells' World Brain, or Bush's Memex, and their shared goal of making all information accessible at one's fingertips, inevitably the response would be, "And now we have that in Google!"

But do we? For most common information-seeking, Google is indeed useful, and I have turned to Google (and Wikipedia) many times while working on this book. Google makes Internet searching easy and effective. Not content with what was already available on the Internet, Google has increased the amount of information significantly with its Google Books project, which has digitized millions of books from major research libraries around the world. But what part of the world's information is not organized and accessible?

A complete answer to that question will depend on who you are and on what we mean by "accessible." Nevertheless, some partial answers are easy. Any information that has not been digitized is not organized and accessible through Google. Google recognizes this problem, and projects like Google Books or the Google News Archive are attempts at a solution. Google has digitized millions of books from large research libraries, but other digitization projects have been less successful. In addition, there is a danger in leaving digitization and archiving in the hands of commercial companies, as scholars learned when Google discontinued its new archive digitization project (Salvucci). Libraries all over the world are digitizing portions of their archives, for example, but the world's archives will most likely never be completely digitized. It's just too expensive for most libraries to do. We can think not only of the archives or large research libraries, but of public libraries and historical societies and associations the world over. We can ask with some seriousness whether we would really want *all* of the world's information organized and accessible, since much of it would never be read or used, but it is a theoretical question that we will never need to answer in practice.

In addition to undigitized information, we can add various kinds of proprietary information. Corporate records are often digitized, but are not accessible through Google or any other public search engine. I have heard firsthand accounts from librarians working with economics undergraduates of the information they expect to be available to them. Many of them expect to be able to find whatever information they want about any company, and it surprises them that corporations do not release all of the information they have about sales, marketing, or technology. Current corporate information will never be completely publicly accessible.

And what do we mean by accessible? Clearly, Google believes that Google Books makes millions of books "accessible." Yes, and no. All of the books in Google Books are *searchable*, but the casual Googler will not be able to read the full text of most books published after 1923 or so because of copyright. Many publishers believe that even digitizing the books and making them searchable is a violation of copyright, resulting in the 2005 class action suit against Google by the Author's Guild and Association of American Publishers. Google would like to make those books more accessible, but for the immediate future the books after 1923 — probably the books people would most want to read — can be read only in fragments. They are available in libraries, and mostly only in print. So, in addition to the economic obstacle of digitizing information, we have the legal obstacle of copyright preventing millions of books from truly being accessible through Google or any other service, not to mention the problems with a commercial entity monopolizing that information.

What is accessible also depends on who you are, or more specifically, with what institutions you are affiliated. Academics (i.e., most of my interlocutors who believed Google had solved the problems of the universal library) tend to look on information as Vannevar Bush did. Information just appears. Books are there in the library, or they can easily be borrowed from other libraries by filling in an online form. Articles, whether from popular magazines or esoteric scholarly journals, are often online and easily accessible. Even in circumstances where the articles are not just delivered to the virtual desktop, as Bush dreamed of, they are available in print somewhere in some library, and can be borrowed.

This is even more true for those who work at universities with very large, well endowed libraries. At the time of writing, I work at a university with one of the largest and richest research libraries in the world. Except for proprietary information and undigitized or unpublished archival materials that exist only in one place, I can get just about whatever information I want on whatever subject. If I want to research particle physics or read a mystery novel from the nineteen forties, I can get what I want. If it has been published or digitized, and is available somewhere in some library, I can probably have it delivered to my library or my email. Google Scholar makes scholarly articles searchable the way Google Books does for books. For most people in the world, using Google Scholar is similar to using Google Books. They can search for articles, but if they click on a link they are asked to pay a hefty fee to read the article. Unlike people without such affiliations, when scholars at institutions with large research libraries use Google Scholar, most of the links work.

At this point a natural response might be, who cares? Most people are not scholars, and as the history of public libraries showed us, they do not want to be scholars. Most people do not want to research deeply into any subjects. So what difference does it make if they cannot get a copy of the *Esoteric Journal of Academic Wankery* or whatever? This objection does have some force, but it misses the point in at least a couple of ways. For one thing, more than scholarly information is difficult to find. Readers who have a taste for genre fiction from the mid-twentieth century, for example, would be just as hard pressed to find the books they want as scholars wanting scientific articles, even were they willing to purchase the books themselves. Many popular books of bygone eras were purchased by public libraries, and then discarded once they were no longer popular. Any unusual taste for books or knowledge, even if not "scholarly" as such, will be left unsated by a market that satisfies only the most popular of tastes. A truly universal library would probably be far more popular than anyone could realize, as esoteric tastes would be allowed to develop freely, much as communities of esoteric tastes can now come together on the Internet.

In addition, a universal library has value even if it were not popular. The Enlightenment goal of a universal library accessible to all is still alive, as we can see in Google's mission statement. But that goal has certainly not been reached. To say that most people do not want to reach that goal in the first place is beside the point. Most people have never wanted to be enlightened. But what of those who do? As Hafner and Sterling-Folker argued, relying strictly upon commercial media for information means that only the most popular and profitable information will be available, whether it comes in the form of books, magazine articles, or even television shows. Is "unless everyone wants it, no one gets it" an appropriate motto for citizens of a democratic republic? And what about those people who want medical information in medical journals but have no access to them? Or who are concerned by the environmental questions of the day and want to go beyond new articles? What about people who are just curious about something and want to read something deeper than a Wikipedia article? Until Google achieves its mission, which is doubtful, the only places for those people to go are libraries. This is not a bad thing, but it does mean that, so far at least, not everything is on the Internet, and that without libraries available to all, the possibility of public enlightenment is nonexistent, rather than just slim.

The Digital Public Library of America

Perhaps the latest articulation of the universal library dream (as of this writing) will be more successful than the World Brain and the Memex. In a December 2010 article in the *New York Review of Books*, Harvard Librarian (and historian of the French Enlightenment) Robert Darnton discussed the effects on the growing commercialization of access to knowledge represented by the Google Books project, and as a counterbalance to this commercialization of such access called for a Digital Public Library of America (DPLA). Such a digital public library could work with Google's holdings or those of the Hathi Trust or strike out on its own and digitize the vast majority of books in the major American research libraries. Theoretically, tens of millions of books and ultimately audiovisual items could be made available to anyone with an Internet connection. It sounds like an ambitious and expensive project, but as Darnton mentions the major obstacle is not the money — despite the significant expense — but the legal issues surrounding copyright, especially for works published between 1923 and 1964 that are considered "orphan works," that is, works that are out of print, but possibly in copyright, sometimes with no known copyright holder to claim the copyright. Though he does not mention it, another problem is the amount of scholarly information — some of it publicly funded — controlled by commercial publishers. Even if the DPLA became a reality, it would not solve all the problems attendant upon the commercialization, Darnton realizes, but "it would open the way to a general transformation of the landscape in what we now call the information society," and create "a new ecology, one based on the public good instead of private gain." Darnton considered his jeremiad "an appeal to change the system" ("Library").

The appeal appeared in tandem with the Digital Public Library Project that emerged from Harvard's Berkman Center for Internet and Society, with funding from the Alfred P. Sloan Foundation. As I write, "the DPLA Steering Committee is leading the first concrete steps toward the realization of a large-scale digital public library that will make the cultural and scientific record available to all" (Digital). The goal may be unattainable, and at the moment there has not been significant enough progress for me to comment on the project, but its success would be the closest thing to a universal library universally available that we have yet seen.

It is no coincidence that Darnton is a scholar of the French Enlightenment and an historian of the *Encyclopédie*, because a Digital Public Library of America would be an example of the Enlightenment project in the domain of information. At a conference of librarians and publishers in November 2011, Darnton spoke about the DPLA and argued that "it is a feasible, affordable project as well as an opportunity to realize the Enlightenment goals on which our republic was founded" (Darnton "Digital"). He explicitly invoked the metaphor of enlightenment, beginning with a quotation from Thomas Jefferson: "He who receives an idea from me, receives instruction himself without lessening mine; as he who lights his taper at mine, receives light without darkening me" (Jefferson 1291). Darnton equated the DPLA with the lit taper enlightening the world through the availability of ideas. Immediately after this passage, Jefferson argues that "invention then cannot, in nature, be a subject of property," but only of rights, which are granted "according to the will and convenience of the society."

Article 1, Section 8 of the United States Constitution, which Darnton quoted in his speech, states that Congress shall have the power "to promote the Progress of Science and useful Arts, by securing for limited Times to Authors and Inventors the exclusive Right to their respective Writings and Discoveries." This section provides the Constitutional justification for copyright law, but by turning what was meant to be a time-limited right into a perpetual intellectual property right, a society reduces the amount of ideas in circulation and thereby reduces the possibility of sharing and being enlightened by those ideas. The Sonny Bono Copyright Term Extension Act of 1998 extends copyright for works created after January1, 1978 to the life of the author plus 70 years for private authors and "95 years from publication or 120 years from creation, whichever is shorter" for corporate works (U.S. Copyright). Obviously this privileges the rights of corporations over the public good. Darnton argued that "since then, the flame of Jefferson's taper has nearly died out," and that "the time has come to relight Jefferson's taper."

CONCLUSION

The Universal Library *of the* Enlightenment

THE SCIENTIFIC AND POLITICAL principles of the Enlightenment provide the philosophical foundation for American academic and public libraries, and the ultimate goal to which these libraries as a system approach — a universal library available to all — would be the culmination of the Enlightenment project in the domain of information.

In "Technological Change, Universal Access, and the End of the Library," I argued that to plan for the future of libraries, librarians had to think about the end those libraries were to serve, the *telos* of the library, as the Greeks would say. We still need to think teleologically about libraries, but the end or *telos* of libraries is suggested by their origins as well. In this book I have deliberately focused on founding principles, motivating documents, and original inspirations — the beginning rather than the end of libraries — but I also believe that the principles motivating the founding of libraries could suggest a *telos* for libraries. Looking backward is not always reactionary or regressive, because looking to the past can often give us inspiration for the present, as many thinkers during the Renaissance and the Enlightenment periods looked to ancient Greece and Rome for inspiration, or as Americans frequently look back to the United States Constitution and the writings of the American founders. Librarians can do that, too. In our beginning is our end.

Librarians as professionals have an obligation to defend the values of their profession, values originating in the philosophical and political principles of the Enlightenment. Collecting, organizing, and making information accessible to scholars and to citizens of a democratic republic are not values created in a vacuum by librarians, but values dependent upon the broad commitments to intellectual virtues of reason, discovery, invention, classification, understanding, and experiment, as well as to political virtues of intellectual freedom, democracy, liberty, equality, and emancipation inherited from the Enlightenment. In his *Life of Reason*, the philosopher George Santayana wrote that "progress is relative to an ideal which reflection creates" (1). We could measure progress in the future by how close we come to achieving goals derived from the Enlightenment. We look to the past to discover why we do what we do or hold the values we hold, but we can also look to the past and ask whether past values can still motivate present action. Though *how* we do things often changes, the reasons *why* we do them often remain, so to recover those reasons helps us travel more thoughtfully into the future.

American libraries were inspired by the values of the Enlightenment, and protecting those values in the future is our professional obligation. Whatever promotes reason, understanding, intellectual freedom, and the free flow of information is to be defended; whatever hinders these opposed. Whether we are talking about fighting a challenge to a controversial book in a public library or a commercial copyright challenge to the circulation of scholarly information, the reasons for doing so are the same. Librarians have a necessary role to play in supporting these Enlightenment values, a role that goes beyond being neutral technicians dispensing information. Even a perfect digital library of all the world's information would require librarians to organize it and to help people discover the useful knowledge therein. Our far from perfect system of libraries requires much more from librarians. They must be more than neutral technicians organizing information, but also agents of enlightenment.

Librarians often consider themselves to be neutral providers of information, never taking sides in controversies, but they also are champions of intellectual freedom, and the American Library Association even has a dedicated Office of Intellectual Freedom. However, intellectual freedom is a value at odds with librarian neutrality. The implication of my argument is that librarians cannot be, and should not be, neutral at all. Intellectual freedom should not mean the freedom to believe nonsense, but only to read it. And as proponents of intellectual freedom, librarians are by default implicated in the entire scheme of Enlightenment values I have elaborated. Espousing a belief in intellectual freedom without also espousing a belief in critical reason, individual liberty, and emancipation from intolerance and bigotry results in philosophical incoherence. Intellectual freedom does mean that libraries should provide all information to all people, but it does *not* mean that librarians have to remain neutral towards that information, or believe or act as if all information is equal. Librarians can be critical towards information without restricting access to it.

I have discussed the universal library both as a dream and a practical goal, and I believe that a truly universal library would be the culmination of the Enlightenment regarding the accessibility of knowledge. Even if it is an impractical dream, it is one that American libraries have worked hard to make come true, with their collections, their robust network of sharing, and their attempts to organize the chaos of information and help people find it. The closer we move to that dream, the better off our democratic society is.

Though they are distinct agencies in many ways, both academic and public libraries exist to connect people with information. This is a common definition of what libraries do, but I think it is too narrow. In the examples of libraries we have seen, both academic and public, some larger purpose emerges. Libraries exist to educate, or to allow people to educate themselves, and even public libraries were founded as educational rather than recreational institutions. Education remains too narrow a function, though, even for academic libraries. Perhaps we can borrow from Lowell Martin the idea that libraries exist for education and enrichment. Ideally, visiting or using a library means more than that people will be better informed; it means people will be *better people*. A major goal of the Enlightenment was to improve the lives of everyone, and the values we have discussed were meant as means to that end. Libraries exist to improve people's lives in ways related to, but not restricted to, information. A truly universal library would go furthest towards that education and enrichment.

A universal library, the Universal Library of the Enlightenment we might call it, would also be much broader than the text-centered libraries discussed throughout much of the book. Though reading and books in some format should always hold a central place of importance in libraries, technological improvements have supplemented books and reading while serving similar purposes, and libraries have long provided audiovisual as well as reading materials. Some critics decry this, and even now call for libraries to promote "serious reading," but to most librarians it would seem obvious that a documentary or feature film can serve the same purpose as a many books, either for education or enrichment. The historical sources I have mentioned almost always thought of libraries in terms of books, but a truly universal library would collect and make available what we could call the cultural record, or even the human record, every document and artifact of human creation that could possibly be collected and made accessible.

The Universal Library of the Enlightenment would include books and films and music and make those available to all regardless of their means. However, this does not mean there must be only *one* universal library, which is the implication of the universal library schemes discussed in the previous chapter. The universal library is a useful metaphor, but what matters is the system of libraries and how they work together to provide universal access to the human record. The Digital Public Library of America will work along this model. Just because everything is not digitized and available through the Internet — and likely never will be — does not mean a universal library is impossible. As I have argued, for many academics, something like a universal library is already in place, especially for purely scholarly information.

Over the course of the book, we have encountered numerous values associated with the Enlightenment relevant to libraries in one way or another: the primacy of reason, the benefits of scientific investigation, the freedom of thought and speech, the freedom to study and learn, the freedom to publish what you want, the rule of law, the equality of citizens in a republic, and the necessity of providing those equal citizens with equal opportunities for education and even enrichment. Whatever the burdens of the Enlightenment project — and there have been many — the benefits have been substantial, and the goal has always been to emancipate human beings from the restrictions imposed by nature, or oppressive religious dogma, or tyrannical governments, and to improve the lives of human beings in every way possible, to make each human life as worthwhile and enjoyable as it can be without regard to wealth or status or creed. This emancipation and improvement takes many forms, from healthcare to sanitation to parks and museums, and libraries have always played their part in that.

The Universal Library of the Enlightenment is a real possibility, and to some extent already exists through the system of American libraries and the librarians who manage them. Further progress toward the universal library goal faces dangers, of course. As I write, book publishers still struggle to create a sustainable model of publishing ebooks that includes libraries; public library budgets have received deep cuts during a recession; academic libraries struggle to pay for the rising cost of scientific journals; school libraries have lost their librarians in some parts of the country. The digital technology that has the potential to revolutionize access to information has instead revolutionized the commercial ability to control that information, to the point where libraries often do not own, and thus cannot assure preservation of and perpetual access to, a goodly amount of their digital collections.

CONCLUSION

As I mentioned in the beginning, the Enlightenment project itself is always in danger. Schools in some states are allowed to teach biblical creationism in science classes, under the guise of "intelligent design." The Governor of Texas, who announced his candidacy for the Presidency as I was finishing this book, told the public that "there is hope for America. It lies in heaven, and we will find it on our knees," a claim immensely at odds with the American founding of an enlightened republic and the pragmatic spirit of American development (Memoli). When asked by a nine-year-old boy how old the earth was, the same candidate responded thus: "How old do I think the earth is. You know what, I don't have any idea. I know it's pretty old — so it goes back a long long ways. I'm not sure anybody actually knows completely and absolutely how long ago the earth is," a claim that would certainly surprise most scientists. The governor is saved only by his qualifiers *completely* and *absolutely*. His understanding of evolution is no greater: "Your mom is asking about evolution. You know, that's a theory that's out there; it's got some gaps in it. In Texas, we teach both creationism and evolution in our public schools — because I figure you're smart enough to figure out which one is right" (Drum). An incoherent but aggressive anti-government political movement has proponents who often claim they want to "take back America," but who seem to want to take America back to the nineteenth century. Combined with the growing disparity of wealth in the country, we are perhaps in danger of a return to the Gilded Age, an age gilded for the wealthy considerably more than for the rest. Indeed, it comes as no surprise to me that the philanthropic philosophy espoused by Andrew Carnegie finds a contemporary voice in Bill Gates and Warren Buffett, as the gap between the wealthy and the rest approaches nineteenth century standards.

We must remember that libraries and the Enlightenment have *always* been endangered. A crisis always exists, and the current generation merely believes the crisis is new. There have been aggressively ignorant populist parties throughout American history. Libraries and public educational institutions of all sorts have been chronically underfunded, then defunded in rough financial times. The country may be dividing politically along regional lines, but that division is unlikely to result in another Civil War. The Gilded Age was an age of hardship for many Americans, but a progressive movement rose to systematically improve those conditions. There has never been a perfect age, and the struggle for the enlightenment, emancipation, and enrichment of the lives of most will of necessity be a continuous fight, and there might be no final victory.

In the midst of this, libraries and the Enlightenment project both continue their struggle. With all of the ignorance, hatred, bigotry, violence, poverty, insecurity, and uncertainty in the country, both libraries and the Enlightenment can still provide hope for better days. Libraries are still places where people can find enlightenment, education, and enrichment. They are not warehouses for old books, as some people think, but active, thriving places where ideas clash and cultures engage, where values other than the strictly commercial survive and inspire, places people can go, physically or virtually, and emerge better people, their lives improved and through them perhaps our society improved. Extending or maintaining that possibility for all people equally, however achieved, remains a goal and a triumph for libraries and the Enlightenment.

BIBLIOGRAPHY

7 U.S.C. § 304 : US Code - Section 304: Investment of Proceeds of Sale of Land or Scrip. Web. 25 July 2011.

Abbot, George, and. *A Short History of the Library Company of Philadelphia. Compiled from the Minutes, Together with Some Personal Reminiscences, by George Maurice Abbot.* Philadelphia: Library Company of Philadelphia, 1913. Print.

American Library Association. *Libraries and Adult Education.* Chicago: American Library Association, 1926. Print.

Americans for Truth about Homosexuality. "Sarah Palin, 'Daddy's Roommate' and the Left's Hypocrisy on 'Book Banning.'" 18 Sept. 2006. Web. 23 Nov. 2011.

Anderson, R. D. *European Universities from the Enlightenment to 1914.* Oxford: Oxford University Press, 2004. Print.

At the Instance of Benjamin Franklin: A Brief History of the Library Company of Philadelphia. Revised and enlarged edition. Philadelphia: Library Company of Philadelphia, 1995. Online.

Bailyn, Bernard, ed. *The Debate on the Constitution: Federalist and Antifederalist Speeches, Articles, and Letters During the Struggle over Ratification.* New York: Library of America, 1993. Print.

Bivens-Tatum, Wayne. "Technological Change, Universal Access, and the End of the Library." *Library Philosophy and Practice* 9.1 (2006). Online.

Blackwell, Albert. *Friedrich Schleiermacher and the Founding of the University of Berlin : The Study of Religion as a Scientific Discipline.* Lewiston: E. Mellen Press, 1991. Print.

Blair, Ann. "Reading Strategies for Coping with Information Overload Ca. 1550-1700." *Journal of the History of Ideas* 64.1 (2003). Print.

———. *Too Much to Know : Managing Scholarly Information before the Modern Age.* New Haven: Yale University Press, 2010. Print.

Blom, Philipp. *Enlightening the World : Encyclopédie, the Book That Changed the Course of History.* New York: Palgrave Macmillan, 2005. Print.

Bobinski, George. *Carnegie Libraries: Their History and Impact on American Public Library Development.* Chicago: American Library Association, 1969. Print.

Bombardieri, Marcella. "Summers' Remarks on Women Draw Fire." *Boston.com.* 17 Jan 2005. Web. 20 July 2011.

Boston Public Library. "Upon the Objects to Be Attained by the Establishment of a Public Library: Report of the Trustees of the Public Library of the City of Boston 1852." 1852. Web. 29 July 2011.

Bostwick, Arthur, ed. *The Library and Society.* New York: H. W. Wilson Company, 1920. Print.

Bowker, Geoffrey C., and Susan Leigh Star. *Sorting Things Out: Classification and Its Consequences.* Cambridge, MA: MIT Press, 1999. Print.

Boyer, Ernest. "Schleiermacher, Shaftesbury, and the German Enlightenment." *The Harvard Theological Review* 96.2 (2003): 181-204. Print.

Bush, Vannevar, and James M. Nyce. *From Memex to Hypertext : Vannevar Bush and the Mind's Machine.* Boston: Academic Press, 1991. Print.

Canfora, Luciano. *The Vanished Library.* Berkeley: University of California Press, 1989. Print.

Carnegie, Andrew. *The Gospel of Wealth, and Other Timely Essays.* New York: Century, 1901. Print.

Cassirer, Ernst. *The Philosophy of the Enlightenment.* Princeton: N.J. Princeton University press, 1951. Print.

Casson, Lionel. *Libraries in the Ancient World.* New Haven: Yale University Press, 2001. Print.

"Center for Research Libraries - History of CRL." Web. 28 July 2011.

Clarke, Jack A. "Gabriel Naudé and the Foundations of the Scholarly Library." *The Library Quarterly* 39.4 (1969): 331-343. Print.

Clarke, Michael. "Kant's Rhetoric of Enlightenment." *The Review of Politics* 59.1 (1997): 53-73. Print.

Cocalis, Susan L. "The Transformation of 'Bildung' from an Image to an Ideal." *Monatshefte* 70.4 (1978): 399-414. Print.

Columbia University Libraries. "History of Collections." Web. 30 Aug 2011.

Commager, Henry Steele. *The Empire of Reason: How Europe Imagined and America Realized the Enlightenment*. Garden City, N.Y: Anchor Press/Doubleday, 1977. Print.

Darnton, Robert. "A Library without Walls." *NYRblog*. Web. 20 July 2011.

———. *The Business of Enlightenment : A Publishing History of the Encyclopédie, 1775-1800*. Cambridge: Belknap Press, 1979. Print.

———. "The Digital Public Library of America: The Idea and Its Implementation." Charleston Conference XXXI. Charleston, SC: November 3, 2011.

———. "The Library: Three Jeremiads." *The New York Review of Books* 23 Dec 2010. Web. 13 Aug 2011.

Dewey, Melvil. "The Profession." *The American Library Journal* 30 Sept. 1876: 5-6. Online.

Diderot, Denis. "Encyclopedia (Philosophy)." *The Encyclopedia of Diderot & d'Alembert: Collaborative Translation Project* 635-648A. Web. 20 July 2011.

———. "Political Authority (Autorite Politique)." *The Encyclopedia of Diderot & d'Alembert: Collaborative Translation Project* 635-648A. Web. 20 July 2011.

"Digital Library of America Project." Web. 13 Aug 2011.

Ditzion, Sidney. *Arsenals of a Democratic Culture: A Social History of the American Public Library Movement in New England and the Middle States from 1850 to 1900*. Chicago: American Library Association, 1947. Print.

Drake, Miriam, ed. "Association of Research Libraries." *Encyclopedia of Library and Information Science*: 205-217. Print.

Drum, Kevin. "Quote of the Day: How Old Is the Earth?" *Mother Jones*. Web. 25 Aug 2011.

Dudley, Will. *Understanding German Idealism*. Stocksfield, U.K.: Acumen, 2008. Print.

DuMont, Rosemary. *Reform and Reaction: the Big City Public Library in American Life*. Westport, Conn: Greenwood Press, 1977. Print.

Fallon, Daniel. *The German University: a Heroic Ideal in Conflict with the Modern World*. Boulder, Colo: Colorado Associated University Press, 1980. Print.

Fichte, Johann. *The Purpose of Higher Education : Also Known as the Vocation of the Scholar*. Mt. Savage Md.: Nightsun Books, 1988. Print.

Fischer, Hans. "Conrad Gessner (1516–1565) as Bibliographer and Encyclopedist." *The Library* s5-XXI.4 (1966): 269-281. Print.

Flanagan, Maureen. *America Reformed: Progressives and Progressivisms, 1890s-1920s*. New York: Oxford University Press, 2007. Print.

Foucault, Michel. *Discipline and Punish: The Birth of the Prison.* New York: Pantheon Books, 1977. Print.

———. "What is Enlightenment?" *Ethics: Subjectivity and Truth.* New York: New Press, 1997. Print.

Franklin, Benjamin. *Autobiography of Benjamin Franklin.* Philadelphia, PA: J. B. Lippincott & Co., 1869. Print.

French, John. *A History of the University Founded by Johns Hopkins.* Baltimore: Johns Hopkins Press, 1946. Print.

Fukuyama, Francis. *The End of History and the Last Man.* New York: Free Press, 1992. Print.

Gay, Peter. *The Enlightenment: An Interpretation.* New York: Knopf, 1966. Print.

Godwin, William. *Enquiry Concerning Political Justice, and Its Influence on Morals and Happiness.* 1st Amer. from the 2nd London ed. corr ed. Philadelphia: Printed by Bioren and Madan, 1796. Print.

Google. "Google Investor Relations: Frequently Asked Questions." Web. 23 Nov. 2011.

Graham, Hugh Davis, and Nancy Diamon. *The Rise of American Research Universities: Elites and Challengers in the Postwar Era.* Baltimore: Johns Hopkins University Press, 1997. Print.

Gregory, Frederick. "Kant, Schelling, and the Administration of Science in the Romantic Era." *Osiris* 5 (1989): 17-35. Print.

Hadley, Chalmers, ed. *Why Do We Need a Public Library?: Material for a Library Campaign.* Chicago: American Library Association, 1910. Print.

Hafner, Arthur. *Democracy and the Public Library : Essays on Fundamental Issues.* Westport Conn.: Greenwood Press, 1993. Print.

Hamlin, Arthur. *The University Library in the United States, Its Origins and Development.* Philadelphia: University of Pennsylvania Press, 1981. Print.

Harris, Michael. *The Role of the Public Library in American Life : A Speculative Essay.* Champaign: University of Illinois Graduate School of Library Science, 1975. Print.

Henderson, John. *Thomas Jefferson's Views on Public Education.* London: G. P. Putnam's Sons, 1890. Print.

Hofstadter, Richard, and Wilson Smith, eds. *American Higher Education: a Documentary History, Vol. 2*. Chicago: University of Chicago Press, 1961. Print.

BIBLIOGRAPHY

Horkheimer, Max, and Theodor Adorno. *Dialectic of Enlightenment : Philosophical Fragments.* Stanford: Stanford Univ. Press, 2006. Print.

Humboldt, Wilhelm. *Humanist without Portfolio: an Anthology of the Writings of Wilhelm Von Humboldt.* Detroit: Wayne State University Press, 1963. Print.

"Iran: Judiciary Official Says Woman to Be Stoned for Husband's Murder, Not Just Adultery." *Los Angeles Times* 12 July 2010.

Israel, Jonathan. *Radical Enlightenment: Philosophy and the Making of Modernity, 1650-1750.* Oxford: Oxford University Press, 2001. Print.

———. *Enlightenment Contested : Philosophy, Modernity, and the Emancipation of Man, 1670-1752.* Oxford: Oxford University Press, 2006. Print.

———. *A Revolution of the Mind : Radical Enlightenment and the Intellectual Origins of Modern Democracy.* Princeton N.J.: Princeton University Press, 2010. Print.

Jefferson, Thomas. *Writings.* New York: Library of America, 1984. Print.

Joeckel, Carleton, and American Library Association. *A National Plan for Public Library Service.* Chicago: American Library Association, 1948. Print.

Johnson, Alvin Saunders. *The Public Library: A People's University.* New York: American Association for Adult Education, 1938. Print.

Johnson, Samuel. *The Yale Edition of the Works of Samuel Johnson, Volume X.* New Haven, CT: Yale Univ. Press, 1977. Print.

Kant, Immanuel. *Prolegomena to Any Future Metaphysics that will be able to come Forward as Science.* Indianapolis: Hackett Pub. Co., 1977. Print.

———. *The Conflict of the Faculties = Der Streit Der Fakultäten.* New York N.Y.: Abaris Books, 1979. Print.

Kelley, Grace O. "The Democratic Function of Public Libraries." *The Library Quarterly* 4.1 (1934): 1-15. Print.

Kramnick, Isaac. *The Portable Enlightenment Reader.* New York: Penguin Books, 1995. Print.

Kwiek, Marek. "Revisiting the Classical German Idea of the University (On the Nationalization of the Modern Institution)." *Polish Journal of Philosophy* 2.1 (2008): 1-24. Print.

Kyrillidou, Martha, and Les Bland, eds. *ARL Annual Salary Survey 2009–2010.* Washington, DC: Association of Research Libraries, 2010. Print.

Lawler, Edwina. "Neohumanistic-Idealistic Concepts of a University." *Friedrich Schleiermacher and the Founding of the University of Berlin : The Study of Religion as a Scientific Discipline.* Lewiston: E. Mellen Press, 1991. 1-44. Print.

Lemay, Joseph. *Printer and Publisher : 1730-1747.* Philadelphia: University of Pennsylvania Press, 2006. Print.

Liebel, Helen P. "The Enlightenment and the Rise of Historicism in German Thought." *Eighteenth-Century Studies* 4.4 (1971): 359-385. Print.

Lucas, Christopher J. *American Higher Education: a History.* New York: St. Martin's Press, 1994. Print.

"Map of the System of Human Knowledge." *The Encyclopedia of Diderot & d'Alembert: Collaborative Translation Project* 635-648A. Web. 20 July 2011.

Martin, Lowell A. *Enrichment : A History of the Public Library in the United States in the Twentieth Century.* Lanham, Md.: Scarecrow Press, 1998. Print.

May, Henry Farnham. *The Enlightenment in America.* New York: Oxford University Press, 1976. Print.

Memoli, Michael A. "Rick Perry Makes High-profile Call for Prayer as He Weighs White House Run." *Los Angeles Times,* 5 Aug 2011. Web. 25 Aug 2011.

Murray, Christopher John, ed. *Encyclopedia of the Romantic Era, 1760-1850.* New York; London: Fitzroy Dearborn, 2004. Print.

Naudé, Gabriel. *Advice on Establishing a Library.* Berkeley: University of California Press, 1950. Print.

O'Hara, Kieron. *The Enlightenment: a Beginner's Guide.* Oxford: Oneworld, 2010. Print.

Ortega y Gasset, José. "The Mission of the Librarian." The Antioch Review 21.2 (1961): 133. Print.

Osborne, Thomas. "The Ordinariness of the Archive." *History of the Human Sciences* 12.2 (1999): 51-64. Print.

Outram, Dorinda. *The Enlightenment.* 2nd ed. Cambridge: Cambridge University Press, 2005. Print.

"Princeton University Library | Library History." Web. 28 July 2011.

Rawls, John. *Political Liberalism.* Expanded ed. New York: Columbia University Press, 2005. Print.

Rayward, W. "H.G. Wells's Idea of a World Brain: A Critical Reassessment." *Journal of the American Society for Information Science* 50.7 (1999): 557-573. Print.

"ReCAP: The Research Collections and Preservation Consortium." Web. 28 July 2011.

"Reports on the Course of Instruction in Yale College by a Committee of the Corporation and the Academical Faculty." New Haven: Yale College, 1828. Web. 25 July 2011.

Röhrs, Herman. *The Classical German Concept of the University and Its Influence on Higher Education in the United States*. Frankfurt am Main: P. Lang, 1995. Print.

Rudy, Willis. *The Universities of Europe, 1100-1914 : A History*. Rutherford, NJ: Fairleigh Dickinson University Press, 1984. Print.

Rüegg, Walter, ed. *Universities in the Nineteenth and Early Twentieth Centuries (1800-1945)*. Cambridge, UK: Cambridge University Press, 2004. Print.

Salvucci, Richard J. "How Google Disrespected Mexican History." *Blog De La AMHE*. Web. 16 Aug 2011.

Santayana, George. *The Life of Reason: or, the Phases of Human Progress*. New York: Charles Scribner's Sons, 1905. Print.

Schelling, Friedrich. *On University Studies*. Ed. Norbert Guterman. Trans. E.S. Morgan. Athens: Ohio University Press, 1966. Print.

Schleiermacher, Friedrich. *Occasional Thoughts on Universities in the German Sense: With an Appendix Regarding a University Soon to Be Established (1808)*. Ed. and Trans. Terrence Tice and Edwina Lawler. San Francisco: EM Text, 1991. Print.

Schlup, Leonard C., and Stephen H Paschen. *Librarianship in Gilded Age America: An Anthology of Writings, 1868-1901*. Jefferson, N.C: McFarland & Co, 2009. Print.

Schmidt, James, ed. *What Is Enlightenment?: Eighteenth-Century Answers and Twentieth-Century Questions*. Berkeley: University of California Press, 1996. Print.

Shera, Jesse. *Foundations of the Public Library: the Origins of the Public Library Movement in New England, 1629-1855*. Chicago: University of Chicago press, 1949. Print.

Shiflett, Orvin. *Origins of American Academic Librarianship*. Norwood N.J.: Ablex Pub. Corp., 1981. Print.

Silver, Brian L. *The Ascent of Science*. Oxford University Press, 1998. Print.

Stewart, Matthew. *The Courtier and the Heretic*. New York: Norton, 2006. Print.

Thelin, John. *A History of American Higher Education*. Baltimore: Johns Hopkins University Press, 2004. Print.

Todorov, Tzvetan. *In Defence of the Enlightenment.* London: Atlantic, 2010. Print.
U.S. Copyright Office. "Copyright Basics." Web. 23 November 2011.
U.S. Department of Education Institute of Education Sciences, National Center for Education Statistics. "Academic Libraries: 2008." 2010. Web. 8 July 2011.
Wells, H. G. *World Brain.* London: Methuen & Co, 1938. Print.
Wiegand, Wayne. *Irrepressible Reformer: A Biography of Melvil Dewey.* Chicago: American Library Association, 1996. Print.
———. *Leaders in American Academic Librarianship, 1925-1975.* Pittsburgh: Beta Phi Mu, 1983. Print.
Williams, Patrick. *The American Public Library and the Problem of Purpose.* New York: Greenwood Press, 1988. Print.
Yeo, Richard R. *Encyclopaedic Visions: Scientific Dictionaries and Enlightenment Culture.* Cambridge: Cambridge University Press, 2001. Print.
———. "A Solution to the Multitude of Books: Ephraim Chambers's 'Cyclopaedia' (1728) as 'The Best Book in the Universe'." *Journal of the History of Ideas* 64.1 (2003): 61-72. Print.

INDEX

Abbot, Ezra, 86
Addams, Jane, 113
Adorno, Theodor, *Dialectic of Enlightenment*, 24–27
adult education, 126–129
   definition of, 126
   movement, 126, 128
   problems with, 127–129
   public library support of, 128
Advice on Establishing a Library (Naudé), 149
Alembert, Jean Le Rond d', 155, 156, 158
   introduction to *Encyclopédie*, 9
American Association of Adult Education, 128
American Library Association (ALA)
   Commission on the Library and Adult Education, 126–129
   efforts of, 119–133
   founding of, 82, 119
   motto of, 102
   National Plan for Libraries (1934), 127–128
   National Plan for Public Library Service (1948), 130–131
   Office of Intellectual Freedom, 187
   support of adult education, 126–129
   support of public libraries, 120–123
   Why Do We Need a Public Library, 120–128
American Philosophical Society, 11
The American Public Library and the Problem of Purpose (Williams), 135
Americans for Truth about Homosexuality, 132
American Society for Promoting Useful Knowledge, 11
Aristarchus, 144
Aristophanes, 144
Arsenals of a Democratic Culture (Ditzion), 94
The Ascent of Science (Silver), 4–5
Ashurbanipal, 146
Association of American Publishers, 178
Association of Research Libraries (ARL), Farmington Plan, 89–90

Author's Guild, 178
Autobiography of Benjamin Franklin, 96
autonomy, 32–37
 religion and, 32–33

Bacon, Francis, 9
Beiser, Frederick, 49, 51
Berkman Center for Internet and Society, 181
Beyme, Karl Friedrich von, 63–64. See also University of Berlin
Bibliotheca Universalis (Gessner), 147–148
Bibliothèque universelle des historiens (Du Pin), 149
Blom, Philipp, 157, 158, 161
 Enlightening the World, 155
Bobinski, George, 117
Boston Public Library, 103–114
 cooperative collections and, 88
 founding of, 103–104, 110–111
 immigrants and, 110, 112–114
 "Report of the Trustees" (1852). See Report of the Trustees of the Public Library of the City of Boston, 1852
Boyer, Earnest, 61–62
Burke, Edmund, *Reflections on the Revolution in France*, 22
Bush, Vannevar, 171–175. See also Memex
 H. G. Wells and, 172–174
 information overload and, 172
The Business of Enlightenment: a Publishing History of the Encyclopédie, 1775-1800 (Darnton), 40, 156–157

Butterfield, Herbert, *The Whig Interpretation of History*, 38–39

Callimachus, 145
Carnegie, Andrew, 114–119
 "The Best Fields for Philanthropy", 116–117
 charity and, 116
 communism and, 115
 death taxes and, 114–115
 "The Gospel of Wealth", 114–115
 philanthropy and, 114
 private property and, 115
 public libraries and, 116–117
Carnegie Corporation, 128
Carnegie Libraries, 114–119
 criticism of, 117–119
Casson, Lionel, *Libraries in the Ancient World*, 145, 146
Catholic Church, criterion for truth, 4
Center for Research Libraries (CRL), 89
Chambers, Ephraim, *Cyclopaedia*, 155
The Classical German Concept of the University and Its Influence on Higher Education in the United States (Röhrs), 61
classification schemes, 11–12, 28–30, 83–84
 of Benjamin Franklin, 98
collection development, 85, 143
 cooperative, 88–90
 Library at Alexandria and, 143
Columbia University Library

INDEX

cooperative collections and, 88, 90
Melvil Dewey and, 83, 86
Commager, Henry Steele, 83
Empire of Reason, 11
communism, 36–37, 115
Condorcet, Marquis de, 6
Conflict of the Faculties (Kant), 53–55, 57–58, 67
conservatism, 14, 24, 49, 112–113
The Constitution of the United States of America
   Article 1, Section 8, 182–183
   copyright law and, 182–183
   debate over, 100
   Enlightenment origins of, 13
   rights and, 13
   slavery and, 16–17
Copernicus, 4–5
copyright, 181, 182–183
   Google and, 177–178
Cornell, Ezra, 72–73
Cornell University, 70
   Andrew White and, 71, 72–73
   challenges to, 73–74
   founding of, 72–73
   German model and, 48, 72–74
   James Morgan Hart and, 70
   libraries and, 84
   motto of, 72
The Courtier and the Heretic (Stewart), 33
Critique of Pure Reason (Kant), 25–26
Crunden, Frederick Morgan, 122–124
Cutter, Charles, 86
   Rules for a Printed Dictionary and Catalogue, 83

"taste elevation theory" and, 109
Cyclopaedia (Chambers), 155

Darnton, Robert
   The Business of Enlightenment, 40, 156–157
   Digital Public Library of America and, 181–184
   Encyclopédie and, 156–157
Declaration of Independence, political enlightenment and, 12–13
"Declaration of the Rights of Man and the Citizen", 13–17
"Declaration of the Rights of Woman and the Female Citizen", 20–21
Descartes, Rene, 9
Dewey Decimal System, 83
Dewey, Melvil, Columbia College Library and, 86–87
Dialectic of Enlightenment: Philosophical Fragments (Horkheimer and Adorno), 25–27
Diamond, Nancy, *The Rise of American Research Universities*, 82
Diderot, Denis, 7–8. See also *Encyclopédie, ou dictionnaire raisonné des sciences, des arts et des métiers*
   Encyclopédie and, 154–162
   imprisonment of, 160
   information overload and, 148
Didymus, 145
Digital Public Library of America (DPLA), 181–184

copyright and, 181
Dionysius Thrax, 145
Discipline and Punish (Foucault), 28
Ditzion, Sidney, 104
  Arsenals of a Democratic Culture, 94
Dudley, Will, 50–51
DuMont, Rosemary, *Reform and Reaction*, 110, 112
Du Pin, Louis Ellies, *Bibliothèque universelle des historiens*, 149

education. *See* adult education; *See also* public education; *See also* public libraries: educational function of
Eliot, Charles W., 71, 74–79. *See also* Harvard University
Harvard University and, 74–75, 78–79
emancipation. *See* autonomy
Empire of Reason: How Europe Imagined and America Realized the Enlightenment (Commager), 11
Encyclopedic Visions (Yeo), 154, 158
Encyclopédie, ou dictionnaire raisonné des sciences, des arts et des métiers (Diderot), 7, 154–162
  as manifetso of the Enlightenment, 156–157
  as time capsule of the Enlightenment, 158–159
  as universal library, 161–162
  biographies and, 158
  censorship and, 159–160
  Denis Diderot and, 7
  information overload and, 154
  Jean Le Rond d'Alembert and, 9
  origins of, 155–156
  purpose of, 157
The End of History and the Last Man (Fukuyama), 38
Enlightening the World (Blom), 155
The Enlightenment. *See also* Radical Enlightenment
  contemporary views of, 23–43
  critiques of, 28–30
  Declaration of Independence and, 12–13
  definition of, 1–3
  distortions of, 32, 35–36, 62. *See also* Todorov, Tzvetan
  emergence of, 62
  German Idealism and, 48–51
  period, 1–2
Enlightenment Contested: Philosophy, Modernity, and the Emancipation of Man 1670-1752 (Israel), 18–19, 41
"The Enlightenment Project". *See also* philosophical Enlightenment; *See also* political Enlightenment
  disambiguation from The Enlightenment, 2
Enquiry Concerning Political Justice and its Influence on Morals and Happiness (Godwin), 35
Enrichment (Lowell), 130

Farmington Plan, 89–90

Fichte, Johann Gottleib, 51, 52, 56–58, 60
  University of Berlin and, 63–64
Fischer, Hans, 147
Folwell, William Watts, 70
Foucault, Michel, *Discipline and Punish*, 28–30
Foundations of the Public Library (Shera), 94
Franklin, Benjamin, 95–99
  Autobiography, 96
Frederick the Great, 49
freedom to learn. *See* Lernfreiheit (freedom to learn)
freedom to teach. *See* Lehrfreiheit (freedom to teach)
French, John C., 79
French Revolution, 2, 12, 14
Friedrich Wilhelm II, 49
Friedrich Wilhelm III, 63
Fukuyama, Francis, *The End of History and the Last Man*, 38

Gay, Peter, 40, 62
gender, 17
German Idealism. *See also* German model of higher education
  definition of, 51
  higher education and, 51–62
  Immanuel Kant and, 48–51
  origins of, 49–51
  The Enlightenment and, 48–51
German model of higher education
  as graduate schools in the U.S., 59, 70–71, 79, 82
  Cornell University and, 72–74
  German Idealism and, 48–52
  Harvard University and, 74–75, 78–79
  influence in the United States, 48, 68–81
  Johns Hopkins University and, 79–82
  Lehrfreiheit (freedom to teach) and, 67, 70
  Lernfreiheit (freedom to learn) and, 67, 70
  religious education and, 69
  three principles of the, 66–67
  University of Berlin and, 63–68
  University of Michigan and, 71
  "Yale Report" and, 76–80
Gessner, Conrad, 147–148
  Bibliotheca Universalis, 147–148
  information overload and, 148
Gilman, Daniel Coit, 71, 80–82
Godwin, William, *Enquiry Concerning Political Justice*, 35
Google
  accessibility and, 177–178
  as universal library, 175–181
  copyright and, 177–178
  Google Books, 176–177
  Google News Archive, 176
  Google Scholar, 179–180
  lawsuit against, 178
Gouges, Olympe de, 20–21
graduate schools, 59, 70–71, 79, 82
Graham, Hugh, *The Rise of American Research Universities*, 82
Green, Samuel Swett, 87

Gregory, Frederick, 60
Gua de Malves, Jean Paul de, 156

Hafner, Arthur, 136–138
Hamlin, Arthur, 82, 84–87
Harris, Michael, 110–113, 118–119
  The Role of the Public Library in American Life, 110
Hart, James Morgan, 70
Harvard University. See also Eliot, Charles W.
  German model and, 74–75, 78–79
  library, 86
  cooperative collections and, 88
  religious education and, 69
Hewins, Caroline M., 121–122
Hill, Walter B., 71
History of American Higher Education (Thelin), 69
Hopkins, Johns, 71, 79–80. See also Johns Hopkins University
Horkheimer, Max, *Dialectic of Enlightenment*, 24–27
Humboldt, Wilhelm, Freiherr von, 64–67
  The Limits of State Action, 64
  three principles of higher education, 66–67
Humboldtian Model, 64. See also German model of higher education
Hume, David, 50–51

In Defence of the Enlightenment (Todorov), 2, 31–32

information overload, 162–164, 169
  Vannevar Bush and, 172
  Denis Diderot and, 148
  Conrad Gessner and, 148
  Gottfried Leibniz and, 148
  José Ortega y Gasset and, 163
intellectual freedom, 186–188
intellectual property, Thomas Jefferson and, 182–183
interlibrary loan, 87–89
invention, 11
Israel, Jonathan, 40–43. See also *Radical Enlightenment*
  Enlightenment Contested, 18–19, 41
  Radical Enlightenment, 41, 150
  Revolution of the Mind, 41–42

Jefferson, Thomas, 100–103
  intellectual property and, 182–183
  Library of Congress and, 102
Johns Hopkins University
  Daniel Coit Gilman and, 71, 80–82
  founding of, 48, 79, 82
  German model and, 80–83
  intellectual freedom and, 81–82
Johnson, Alvin Saunders, *The Public Library: a People's University*, 128–130
Johnson, Samuel, 39–40
The Junto, 95–96, 98. See also The Library Company of Philadelphia
  influence on public libraries, 96
  membership criteria, 95

Kant, Immanuel, 25–26, 60
  "An Answer to the Question: What is Enlightenment?" 3, 49
  Conflict of the Faculties, 53–55, 57–58, 67
  Critique of Pure Reason, 25–26
  David Hume and, 50–51
  definition of Enlightenment, 3
  exclusion of women and, 19
  German Idealism and, 48–51
  Prolegomena to any Future Metaphysics, 50–51
Kelley, Grace O., 134–135
Kirkland, James H., 71
Kramnik, Isaac, 13–14

Lawler, Edwina, 60
Leaders in American Academic Librarianship: 1925-1975 (Wiegand), 91
Le Breton, André-François, 155–156
Lehrfreiheit (freedom to teach), 67, 70
Leibel, Helen, 62
Leibniz, Gottfried, 148
Lemay, Joseph, 97–98
Lernfreiheit (freedom to learn), 67, 70
Letters Concerning the English Nation (Voltaire), 9
librarians
  as technicians, 128
  neutrality and, 187
  status of, 120
libraries. *See* public libraries
Libraries and Adult Education (American Library Association), 126

Libraries in the Ancient World (Casson), 145
Library at Alexandria, 142–147
  acquisitioning by, 145–146
  as universal library, 145–147
  collection development policy, 143
  destruction of, 152
  founding of, 142
  holdings of, 143
Library at Hattasus, 146
Library at Pergamum, 144
Library Bureau of the United States, 82
The Library Company of Philadelphia, 95–99. *See also* The Junto
  motto of, 99
Library Fairness Project, 132
Library Journal, 82
  first issue, 87, 119
Library of Congress, 102
Life of Reason (Santayana), 186
The Limits of State Action (Humboldt), 64
Locke, John, 18
  Two Treatises on Government, 34
Lucas, Christopher, 68, 70–71

MacIntyre, Alasdair, 171
Martin, Lowell, 130–132
  Enrichment, 130
McCosh, James, 90
Memex, 172–175
  description of, 173–174
Mercantile Library Association, 104
Mills, John, 155
A Modern Utopia (Wells), 168

Morrill Act, 73
multiculturalism, 111–112

National Plan for Public Library Service, 1948 (American Library Association), 130–131
Naudé, Gabriel, 44, 147–154
  Advice on Establishing a Library, 149
Newton, Isaac, 9
New York Public Library, cooperative collections and, 88, 90
Northrup, Cyrus, 70

Oberlin College, 68–69
Occasional Thoughts on Universities in the German Sense (Schleiermacher), 55
On University Studies (Schelling), 56
Ortega y Gasset, José, information overload and, 163
Osborne, Thomas, 150

Pepper, William, 71
perfectibility (human), 35–36
Philitas, 145
philosophical Enlightenment, 2–12
  comparison to historical Enlightenment, 2–3, 18, 20, 22
  definition of, 44
  libraries and, 44–46
political Enlightenment, 12–23
  libraries and, 44–46
Popper, Karl, 158
Priestly, Joseph, 10

Princeton University Library, 90–91
Project Gutenberg, 139
Prolegomena to any Future Metaphysics (Kant), 50–51
Ptolomies, 142–145, 148–149. See also Library at Alexandria
public education, 105–107, 119–120
  importance for democracy, 99–103
public libraries
  economic benefits of, 125–126
  educational function of, 108, 122–128, 130–131. See also herein public libraries: purpose of
  first instances, 103–104
  immigrants and, 112–114
  intellectual freedom and, 153
  irrelevance of, 139
  The Junto and, 96
  market model of, 129–130, 138
  popular books and, 108. See also "taste elevation theory"
  purpose of, 131–132, 133–140. See also herein public libraries: educational function of
Public Libraries in the United States of America: their History, Condition, and Management (United States Bureau of Education), 82
The Public Library: a People's University (Johnson), 128–131

Radical Enlightenment, 41–44. See also Israel, Jonathan

definition of, 41–43
difference from The
  Enlightenment, 18–19, 41
period, 2, 41
*Radical Enlightenment:
  Philosophy and the Making
  of Modernity, 1650-1750*
  (Israel), 41, 44, 150. *See
  also* Radical Enlightenment
*Rapport sur l'Instruction
  Publique, fait au nom du
  Comité de Constitution*
  (Talleyrand-Perigord), 22
Rawls, John, 112
Raymond, John Howard, 70
Rayward, W. Boyd, 167, 168–170
*Reflections on the Revolution in
  France* (Burke), 22
Reform and Reaction
  (DuMont), 110
Report of the Trustees of the
  Public Library of the City of
  Boston, 1852, 105–111
*Reports on the Course of
  Instruction in Yale College
  by a Committee of the
  Corporation and the
  Academical Faculty. See* "Yale
  Report"
*Revolution of the Mind:
  Radical Enlightenment
  and the Intellectual Origins
  of Modern Democracy*
  (Israel), 41–42
rights, 13–20
  women's, 22
*The Rise of American Research
  Universities* (Graham and
  Diamond), 82
Rogers, William B., 71

Röhrs, Herman, 67
*The Classical German Concept
  of the University*, 61
*The Role of the Public Library in
  American Life* (Harris), 110
Roman libraries, 146
*Rules for a Printed Dictionary
  and Catalogue* (Cutter), 83

Santayana, George, *Life of
  Reason*, 186
Schelling, Friedrich, 51–52, 58,
  60
  On University Studies, 56
Schleiermacher, Friedrich, 51–52,
  55–56, 58–59, 60
  *Occasional Thoughts on
  Universities in the German
  Sense*, 55
Schott, Robin May, "The Gender
  of Enlightenment", 17
scientific investigation, emergence
  of, 10–11
Sellius, Godefroy, 155
The Shape of Things to Come
  (Wells), 168
Shepherd, Reverend John H., 68–
  69
Shera, Jesse, 97
  Boston Public Library
  and, 103–104
  *Foundations of the Public
  Library*, 94
Silver, Brian, *The Ascent of
  Science*, 4–5
skepticism, 37–38, 50–51
Sonny Bono Copyright Term
  Extension Act of 1998, 183–
  184

Sorting Things Out: Classification and its Consequences (Bowker and Star), 30
Spinoza, Baruch, 18, 33
  as precursor to the Enlightenment, 2, 41
Sterling-Folker, Jennifer, 136–138
Stewart, Matthew, *The Courtier and the Heretic*, 33
Summers, Laurence, 7–8

Tables of Persons Eminent in Every Branch of Learning together with a List of Their Writings (Callimachus), 145
Talleyrand-Perigord, Charles-Maurice de, *Rapport sur l'Instruction Publique, fait au nom du Comité de Constitution*, 22
Tappan, Henry P., 71–72
"taste elevation theory", 105–110
  criticisms of, 109–110
Thelin, John, *History of American Higher Education*, 69
Ticknor, George, 110–113
Todorov, Tzvetan, 31–36. See also The Enlightenment: distortions of
  In Defence of the Enlightenment, 2, 31–32
Treaty of Tilsit, 63
truth, criterion of, 4–5, 81
Two Treatises on Government (Locke), 34

University of Berlin, 63–68
  as basis for German model of higher education, 64–65
  founding of, 51–52, 61, 63–64

University of Chicago, 79
University of Halle, 63
University of Michigan, German model and, 71–72
University of South Carolina, 69
"Upon the Objects to Be Attained by the Establishment of a Public Library". See Report of the Trustees of the Public Library of the City of Boston, 1852
U.S. Constitution. See The Constitution of the United States of America

Vattemare, Nicholas Marie Alexandre, 104
A Vindication of the Rights of Men (Wollstonecraft), 22
A Vindication of the Rights of Woman (Wollstonecraft), 22
Vinton, Frederick, 90
Voltaire, 18
  Letters Concerning the English Nation, 9

Webster, Noah, 100
The Wellesley Half Dozen, 87–88
Wells, H. G., 162–171
  criticism of, 167–170
  faith in science, 165–166
  information overload and, 162–164, 169
  A Modern Utopia, 168
  The Shape of Things to Come, 168
  World Brain, 168–169. See also World Encyclopedia
The Whig Interpretation of History (Butterfield), 38–39

White, Andrew D., 70–71
  Cornell University and, 72–76
  Why Do We Need a Public Library?: Material for a Library Campaign (American Library Association), 120–128
Wiegand, Wayne, 87
  Leaders in American Academic Librarianship, 91
Wilhelm, Friedrich II, 49
Wilhelm, Friedrich III, 63
Williams, Patrick, 135–136
  The American Public Library and the Problem of Purpose, 135
Winsor, Justin, 86
Wissenschaft (science), definition of, 70
Wollstonecraft, Mary, 22–23
women's rights, 22

World Brain (Wells), 168–169. *See also* World Encyclopedia
World Encyclopedia, 162–171
  copyright and, 165
  criticism of, 167–169
  H. G. Wells' description of, 164
  totalitarian nature of, 168
Wynkoop, Asa, 124, 127

Yale College, 69
"Yale Report", 75–79
  defense of classical education, 76–77
  Lehrfreiheit and, 77
Yeo, Richard, *Encyclopedic Visions*, 154, 158

Zenodotus, 144
Ziff, Larzer, 99

www.ingramcontent.com/pod-product-compliance
Lightning Source LLC
Chambersburg PA
CBHW021353300426
44114CB00012B/1216